Raising Meat Rabbits and Ducks

A Homesteader's Essential Guide to Rabbit Breeding and Care Along With Duck Keeping and Sustainable Farming Practices

Table of Contents

Part 1: Backyard Meat Rabbits

A Comprehensive Guide to Raising Rabbits for Meat, Including Tips on Choosing a Breed, Building the Coop, and Harvesting

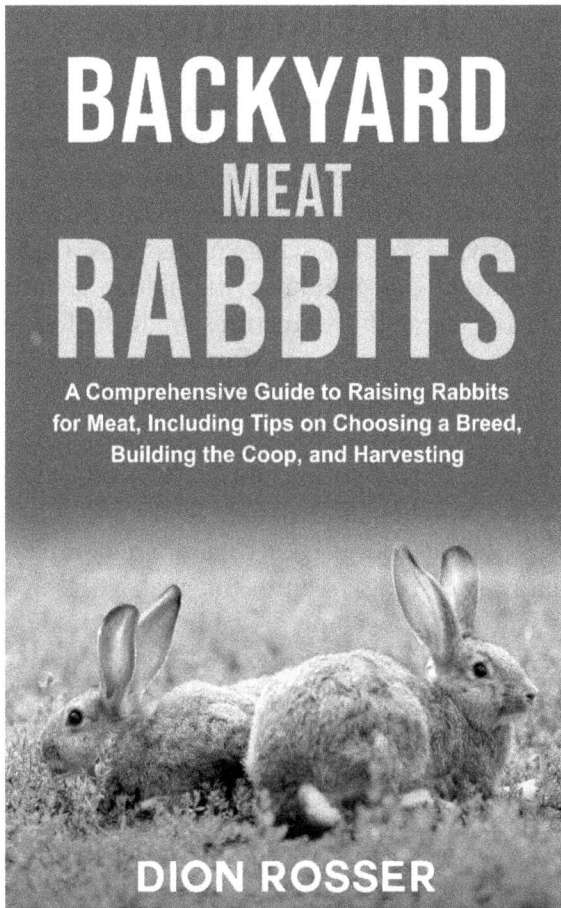

Introduction

Why should you dive headfirst into the world of raising rabbits for meat? There are so many reasons to do so. It's been done forever, yet it's often overlooked. There was a time when rabbits weren't mere domestic companions but a vital part of the homestead's meat production. Long before backyard BBQs became synonymous with sizzling steaks and plump chicken drumsticks, people knew the hidden gem that was rabbits. Once wild and elusive, these fluffy creatures gradually found their place as house pets. It wasn't an overnight transformation, mind you. Before this happened, rabbits were mainly used as a food source.

Now, you may be wondering. Chickens and cows have long been the go-to options for meat, so why go for rabbits? Consider the efficiency of it all. Chickens and cows demand space, feed, and time—a trifecta of valuable resources. Rabbits, on the other hand, are compact powerhouses. They don't require sprawling pastures or massive feed bins. A small corner of your yard can become a rabbit haven and can yield an impressive harvest of tender meat.

And talk about speed. Chickens and cows take their sweet time to mature, demanding your patience while you wait for that perfect moment to savor their flavors. But rabbits? They're the sprinters of the meat world. In a matter of weeks, you'll have rabbit meat on your plate. It's a satisfyingly swift turnaround that even the most hurried homesteader can appreciate, but there's more. Imagine a life where your meat source is not only economical but also sustainable. Rabbits are known for their prodigious breeding abilities, and their swift reproduction cycle ensures a steady supply of meat for your table. While chickens and cows may require more attention to their reproductive needs, rabbits practically write their own script, creating a delightful surplus of meat.

Starting your rabbit adventure comes with various possibilities, and each path has its own goal. There is bound to be one that matches your interests and abilities. Maybe you're aiming for self-sufficiency. Think of having rabbits as a way to create a mini ecosystem. These little creatures can give you good protein to eat. Or perhaps you're into farmers' markets. Rabbit meat may not be the usual choice for some people, but once they taste it, they could become your loyal customers. Another option is connecting with restaurants. Rabbit has become quite popular on menus thanks to creative chefs. By supplying them with quality rabbit meat, you become part of this culinary trend.

However, *keep it real.* Be honest about what you can handle - your skills, time, and resources. Don't get swept up in excitement without a clear goal. There's a story about a family who bought rabbits to eat, but when it was time to process them, they couldn't. They ended up with pets instead of meat. One thing to remember from the start is that raising rabbits for meat means you'll eventually need to deal with harvesting them. It's a serious conversation to have upfront so you know if you're comfortable with the whole process before you even start mating rabbits.

In the world of raising rabbits for meat, your journey may have a different destination, but what ties it all together is your dedication to learning, providing, and maybe even processing rabbit meat. It's about finding your own path and enjoying the adventure along the way.

Chapter 1: Introduction to Backyard Rabbit Farming

Backyard rabbit farming has emerged as a gratifying pursuit for individuals and families looking for a harmonious blend of companionship and sustainable food production. With their docile nature, modest upkeep demands, and prolific breeding tendencies, rabbits have captured the interest of those looking to engage in small-scale animal husbandry. Farming rabbits is a perfect opportunity to cultivate a connection with these endearing creatures while enjoying the benefits of homegrown meat. As the book delves into backyard rabbit raising, it will navigate this venture's various considerations, techniques, and rewards, encompassing everything from selecting suitable rabbit breeds to creating sustainable habitats that fit your lifestyle.

Farming rabbits is a perfect opportunity to cultivate a connection with these endearing creatures while enjoying the benefits of homegrown meat.

Exploring Backyard Rabbit Farming

The realm of backyard rabbit farming is a multi-faceted journey that harmonizes nurturing living beings with sustainable agricultural practices. A fundamental aspect is selecting rabbit breeds that fit in with your goals: meat production, fur, or engaging pets. These decisions lay the foundation for a rewarding experience. It's equally crucial to provide rabbits with appropriate housing space. From cabinets to tractors, the well-being and protection of these animals are paramount considerations. Likewise, attending to their dietary needs with a balanced blend of fresh greens, hay, and nutritionally dense pellets ensures optimal health.

Beyond the practicalities, raising rabbits offers the enriching experience of observing natural behaviors, tending to the growth of rabbit families, and fostering a connection with the rhythms of nature. The benefits extend further, as your garden benefits from the valuable resource of rabbit-waste compost. Moreover, this undertaking encourages a deeper understanding of animal care, husbandry ethics, and sustainable living practices. As you embark on this exploration of backyard rabbit farming, you will find this book will uncover the nuances that make it a fulfilling and educational endeavor for those seeking a connection to the natural world and a pathway to sustainable, self-sufficient living.

Why Raise Backyard Rabbits for Meat

Rabbits have garnered attention as a practical and environmentally conscious option for those seeking an alternative to conventional meat production. Farming rabbits as a source of meat is based on factors like a short reproduction cycle, efficient conversion of feed to protein, and manageable space requirements. These factors have made rabbits a feasible pick for families and individuals aiming to embrace sustainable food practices while making a minimum ecological footprint.

Efficient Feed-to-Meat Conversion Rate

Rabbits stand out for their remarkable efficiency in converting feed into high-quality protein. Known for their herbivorous diet, they have a specialized digestive system that allows them to take the highest amount of nutrition from plant-based materials such as hay and grains. This efficient feed-to-meat conversion rate makes rabbit meat a lean and healthy option. It contributes to resource conservation by minimizing the amount of feed needed to produce a substantial amount of protein.

Minimal Space Requirements

Farming rabbits in your backyard is perfect for people with limited space. Unlike larger domestic animals that demand extensive grazing areas, rabbits can thrive in modest enclosures such as hutches or pens. This adaptability to confined spaces is particularly appealing in urban and suburban settings where land is scarce. Consequently, raising rabbits provides an avenue for meat production even in environments where traditional livestock farming would be impractical.

Rabbits can thrive in modest enclosures such as hutches or pens.
https://pixabay.com/photos/rabbit-hutch-house-easter-cottage-502929/

Dual-Purpose Nature: Meat and Fur

Another compelling facet of rabbit raising is the dual-purpose nature of meat and fur production. Besides providing tender and flavorful meat, certain rabbit breeds' soft and dense fur can be used to make knitted goods like gloves, cardigans, and felts. However, if the fur length is too short, this makes it impossible to make yarn. This dual functionality aligns with sustainable practices by maximizing the yield from each animal, reducing waste, and supporting local artisanal endeavors, choosing rabbits suited to both meat and wool production.

Rapid Reproduction Cycle

The swift reproductive cycle of rabbits contributes to their appeal as a source of meat. A single doe (female rabbit) can produce multiple litters of kits (baby rabbits) each year, resulting in a consistent meat supply. This reproductive efficiency allows for a sustainable and predictable meat production rhythm, reducing the time and resources required to yield a substantial harvest.

Lower Environmental Impact

Rabbit farming dovetails with environmentally conscious practices due to its reduced ecological footprint. Compared to larger livestock, rabbits consume less feed, require smaller living spaces, and generate fewer greenhouse gas emissions. Their efficient resource consumption contributes to conservation efforts by minimizing water usage and land requirements.

Health Benefits

Rabbit meat is considered a healthy protein option because it is a low-fat and low-cholesterol protein. This makes it an appealing choice for people aiming to maintain their weight and cardiovascular health. The lean rabbit meat has a high protein content that encourages muscle health and improves immune function and overall well-being.

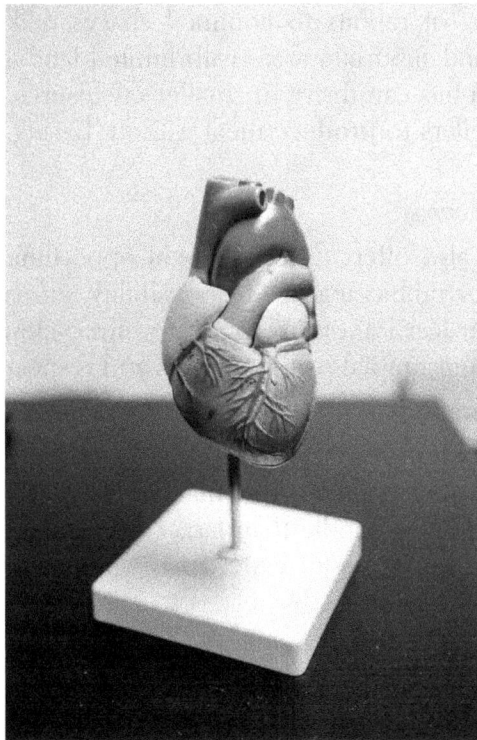

Rabbit meat is an optimal choice for people aiming to maintain their weight and cardiovascular health.
https://unsplash.com/photos/MEbT27ZrtdE

Nutrient-Rich Meat

The meat from rabbits is abundant in essential nutrients that play crucial roles in maintaining metabolic processes. For example, the meat is packed with B vitamins, particularly B12, which is a vital substance required for energy metabolism and nerve function. Likewise, the high iron, zinc, and phosphorus in the meat improves the transport of oxygen in the blood, zinc supports immune system health, and phosphorus improves bone health and cellular function.

Economic Viability

Raising rabbits can be economically practical, making it an accessible option for those looking to produce their own meat. Rabbits grow quickly and efficiently convert feed into meat, resulting in a relatively high protein yield from a modest investment. This efficiency contributes to cost-effective meat production.

Accessibility to Urban Dwellers

The adaptability of rabbits to confined spaces makes them a viable choice for urban and suburban areas with limited land availability. Unlike larger livestock, rabbits can thrive in smaller enclosures. This accessibility enables urban dwellers to produce meat without having to own vast tracts of land.

Educational Value

Rabbit farming also offers an educational opportunity, particularly for children. Caring for rabbits teaches responsibility, empathy, and practical skills. Children can learn about animal care, life cycles, biology, and the importance of treating animals with kindness and respect.

Ethical Considerations

For individuals who prioritize the ethical treatment of animals, raising rabbits aligns with their values. The manageable size of rabbits makes them less intimidating to handle than larger livestock. This can lead to a more humane and less stressful experience when raising and harvesting rabbits for meat and fur.

Reduced Antibiotic Use

Raising rabbits in your backyard involves fewer antibiotics than large-scale commercial meat production. Rabbits are generally hardy animals with fewer health issues, and because of their small size, they get more individualized care, reducing the need for routine antibiotic use.

Local Food Security

Rabbit farming contributes to local food security, ensuring a consistent supply of fresh meat within communities. This localized production decreases dependence on distant food sources during local market supply disruptions, as most rabbit species thrive well in extreme temperatures. This ability to survive in hot and cold temperatures makes rabbits a tremendous alternative meat source. Furthermore, rabbits can adapt to different terrains, making it easier to raise them wherever humans live.

Customized Breeding Programs

Raising rabbits allows breeders to tailor their breeding programs to meet specific goals, whether it's to optimize meat yield and fur quality or adapt to local climates. This customization provides opportunities for experimentation and innovation. Successful breeding programs can further lead to the development of species with better qualities in any of these areas.

Homestead Diversification

For those pursuing a self-sufficient lifestyle, rabbits can be a valuable addition to a diversified homestead. Integrating rabbit husbandry with other practices such as gardening, poultry, and small livestock contributes to a greater variety of resources available for personal consumption.

Hands-on Sustainability

Being such a hands-on and simplified farming activity means that a greater connection is made with the food source, encouraging sustainable practices. Individuals become more mindful of their food consumption and the resources required to produce it, promoting a deeper understanding of sustainability.

Connection to Natural Cycles

When you engage in raising rabbits, this offers insights into the natural cycles of life, reproduction, and responsible animal stewardship. This experience enhances relevant knowledge and awareness of the processes that sustain life and a deeper appreciation for the natural world.

Preservation of Heritage Breeds

Yet another positive for backyard farming is the all-important preservation of genetic diversity and cultural heritage of heritage rabbit breeds. This support for biodiversity safeguards unique breeds from extinction and maintains their historical significance.

Empowerment and Resilience

Rabbit raising empowers small farmers to take control of their food sources and become more self-reliant. Small farmers can produce food and be less dependent on external supply chains while raising rabbits. This process contributes exponentially to personal empowerment.

The decision to consider rabbits as a source of meat embodies a multifaceted approach to sustainable food production. Their efficient feed conversion, minimal space needs, dual-purpose nature, rapid reproduction cycle, and lower environmental impact converge to offer a practical and ethical choice for people seeking to nourish themselves while prioritizing conservation and self-sufficiency responsibly. As an alternative to conventional meat sources, rabbits exemplify how mindful decisions in food production can contribute to a more sustainable and harmonious relationship with the environment.

Addressing Challenges in Backyard Rabbit Farming

Starting your journey on the path to farming rabbit meat has some challenges that require careful attention and proactive management to ensure the well-being of the rabbits and the success of your venture. Here's a detailed exploration of these challenges and how to address them:

Starting your journey on the path to farming rabbit meat has some challenges that require careful attention.

https://unsplash.com/photos/bJhT_8nbUA0

1. Appropriate Housing

Rabbits in their natural habitat are fond of digging underground warrens (tunnels). When raising rabbits in an urban or residential space, it's crucial to provide suitable housing for the rabbits' safety and comfort. Hutches or pens should shield rabbits from predators, provide shelter from weather extremes, and offer proper ventilation. Insulating the housing helps regulate temperature, and correct spacing between wires prevents injuries. Regular cleaning is essential to avoid waste buildup, which leads to health issues and unpleasant odors.

2. Health and Veterinary Care

Maintaining rabbit health requires regular monitoring. Common health concerns in rabbits include digestion issues, dental issues, respiratory infections, and external parasite attacks. Besides conducting regular checkups by yourself, it's better to call in a certified veterinarian who can examine rabbits for signs of illness and behavioral changes and note down changes in diet and stool quality. They are very well-trained to recognize symptoms and provide immediate medical attention to achieve the best results.

3. Meeting Dietary Requirements

Meeting rabbits' dietary needs is vital for their well-being. Their diet should consist of high-quality hay like timothy or orchard grass, fresh vegetables such as leafy greens and carrots, and commercially balanced rabbit pellets. Avoid feeding rabbits foods high in sugar or low in fiber, as these foods can increase toxicity. Ensure access to clean, fresh water at all times to prevent dehydration.

4. Reproduction Management

While rabbits' breeding capacity is advantageous, it must be managed carefully. Uncontrolled breeding can lead to overpopulation, stress, and compromised well-being for rabbits and caretakers. Put into place a breeding plan that you can manage and control. Separate males and females to prevent unintentional breeding.

5. Social and Behavioral Needs

Rabbits are social animals that thrive on companionship. However, introducing rabbits requires a gradual and monitored process to prevent aggression. Housing rabbits alone can lead to loneliness and behavioral problems. Introduce rabbits on neutral territory, monitor interactions, and initially keep them separated in order to avoid conflict.

6. Predator Protection

Rabbits are natural prey animals, making them vulnerable to predators. Secure enclosures with sturdy fencing depending on the predator threat, appropriate wire spacing in fences, and solid barriers help deter predators. Consider adding further predator deterrents like motion-activated lights or noise-making devices.

7. Environmental Enrichment

Rabbits are intelligent and curious creatures that need mental and physical stimulation.

Lack of enrichment can lead to boredom and unwanted behaviors. If you are raising rabbits in an urban space, provide toys like cardboard boxes, create tunnels, and chew toys to keep them occupied. Offer hiding spots, platforms, and opportunities for digging to mimic their natural behaviors.

8. Waste Management

Adequate waste management is crucial to maintaining a healthy living environment. Regularly cleaning soiled areas, cages, and hutches and disposing of waste responsibly are some basic steps for waste management. Incorporating waste management techniques effectively prevents the development of foul odors, reduces the risk of disease transmission, and discourages fly or other pest infestations.

9. Climate Considerations

Extreme temperatures can impact rabbit health. Ensure your housing has adequate ventilation and insulation to prevent heat stress or cold-related health issues. Offer shade in hot weather and warmth in cold weather. Monitoring weather forecasts and making necessary adjustments to their living environment is crucial.

Be sure to offer your rabbits shade in hot weather and warmth in cold weather.
https://www.pexels.com/photo/rural-snowy-village-during-severe-blizzard-4969828/

10. Learning and Adaptation

Raising rabbits is a learning curve, especially for people unfamiliar with animal husbandry. Educating yourself about rabbit care, behavior, and needs through books, online resources, and advice from experienced rabbit owners is best. Be open to adapting your practices based on what works best for your rabbits, as each rabbit species may have unique preferences and requirements. Likewise, the space you keep them in also defines their individual requirements.

11. Parasite Prevention

Regularly inspect your rabbits for signs of external parasite infestation. You'll notice rabbits scratching their fur due to itching, fur loss, or visible pests on their fur. To prevent parasites, always keep their living space ventilated, dry, and clean. Regularly change bedding, clean enclosures, and provide fresh hay. When unsure, don't hesitate to consult a veterinarian for appropriate preventive measures or treatments if necessary.

12. Handling and Socialization

Gentle and positive handling is crucial for rabbits' well-being. When picking up a rabbit, support its hindquarters to avoid injury. Spend time near them, offering treats and gentle strokes. Gradually increase interaction to help them become accustomed to your presence and build trust.

13. Quarantine Procedures

When introducing new rabbits to your existing group, implement a quarantine period of about two to four weeks. This minimizes the risk of introducing diseases. Keep new rabbits separate during this time and monitor their health closely. Consult a veterinarian for guidance on quarantine procedures.

14. Observing Behavior

Regularly check your rabbits' behavior to detect any changes. Rabbits are experts at hiding signs of illness, so any alterations in eating habits, activity levels, grooming, or behavior could indicate underlying health issues. Promptly address any concerning changes.

15. Safety from Chemicals

Rabbits like to nibble on things, so ensure their environment is free from toxic substances and plants. Remove any chemicals, pesticides, or potentially harmful materials from their living area to prevent accidental ingestion.

16. Handling Stress

Sudden changes or disturbances can trigger stress in rabbits. You can minimize stress in these sensitive creatures by providing a stable environment, avoiding loud noises and sudden movements, handling them gently, and limiting prolonged exposure to unfamiliar sounds.

17. Grooming Needs

Long-fur rabbits like Angoras need regular grooming to prevent fur matting and tangling. Not fulfilling their grooming needs will cause discomfort and lead to several other skin issues. It's crucial to understand that the grooming requirements change slightly with every rabbit species. Recognizing and fulfilling these grooming needs is your responsibility as their caretaker. Rabbits with long and thick fur will need more care and attention than short-haired breeds.

18. Fostering Trust

Rabbits are intelligent and can bond with humans caring for them, but it takes time and patience. To foster trust, try spending more time near their enclosure and feed them their favorite snacks once a day. You can offer treats or fresh vegetables by hand to create positive associations. Avoid forcing interaction and allow them to approach you at their own pace.

19. Health Records

Keep accurate health records for each rabbit. Document their medical history, previous treatments, vaccination data, and any health concerns they are suffering from. These records are valuable for tracking their health, discussing concerns with veterinarians, and making informed breeding and care decisions.

20. Community and Resources

Talking with other rabbit enthusiasts through joining local or online communities will benefit you exponentially. You can share your experiences, seek advice from veterans in rabbit farming, and educate yourself on other's expertise. Interacting with experienced rabbit owners will undoubtedly provide valuable insights and support.

21. Time Commitment

Farming rabbits takes time, dedication, and commitment. Your daily tasks will include feeding, cleaning enclosures, monitoring health, and providing social interaction. Be prepared to dedicate time to their care, as neglecting their needs can lead to health issues and poor well-being.

22. Emergency Preparedness

Always be prepared for any medical emergency with a feasible action plan. The plan can include knowing evacuation procedures, providing first aid, and having contact information for a veterinarian knowledgeable about rabbit care. Being prepared ensures a swift response in critical situations.

23. End-of-Life Considerations

Understanding the rabbits' end-of-life needs and acting humanely and responsibly is crucial in rabbit farming. If a rabbit is suffering from a terminal illness or has their health deteriorating rapidly, be prepared to make difficult decisions about euthanasia in consultation with a veterinarian. Have a plan for proper disposal and consider environmentally friendly methods if needed.

By addressing these points, you'll be well-prepared to navigate the challenges of backyard rabbit farming. Taking a proactive and informed approach ensures the well-being of the rabbits and promotes a positive and fulfilling experience for both the caretaker and the rabbits themselves.

Imagine a sustainable food production method that fits into your backyard, offers nutrient-rich meat, and introduces you to a world of unique companionship. Backyard rabbit farming for meat isn't just a venture; it's a journey that connects you to the rhythms of nature, nourishes your curiosity, and enriches your understanding of ethical food sources.

As you step into raising rabbits, you're entering a world where efficiency meets compassion. Discover how these small, cute, and furry creatures have made waves in the culinary industry, having abilities to convert feed into high-quality protein with nutrient-rich deposits. Explore the intricate dance between sustainable practices and responsible stewardship as you embark on a path that transcends traditional meat production methods.

Picture yourself creating tailored living spaces that provide comfort and security for your rabbits, and witness the joy of nurturing lives that, in turn, nourish you. As you explore the details of housing design, health maintenance, and dietary needs, you'll uncover the fascinating intricacies of rabbit care. Each challenge you face becomes an opportunity to deepen your connection with these creatures and enhance their quality of life.

Imagine the satisfaction of taking control of your food source, knowing that the meat on your table has been raised with care and integrity. Backyard rabbit raising isn't just about sustenance; it's a holistic approach that touches upon health benefits, ethical considerations, and the satisfaction of being part of a community of responsible food producers.

The world of rabbit farming invites you to explore beyond the confines of traditional meat consumption. It encourages you to embrace a hands-on, sustainable lifestyle that aligns with nature's rhythms. Whether you're a novice or a seasoned enthusiast, this journey is about fostering a deep connection with the animals you raise, the environment you nurture, and the sustenance you derive from it all.

Are you intrigued to learn more about the art and science of breeding rabbits for meat? Dive into the captivating world of responsible food production, compassionate care, and sustainable living. Discover how the humble rabbit can be a source of culinary delight and a profound connection to the natural world. Your journey into backyard rabbit raising promises a tapestry of experiences that enrich your life while contributing to a healthier planet.

Chapter 2: Choosing the Right Breed for Production

Knowing the right rabbit breed to choose from for your meat production is essential. If you are planning on going into it commercially, it can lead to a lucrative and rewarding business venture. Since no two breeds of rabbits are the same based on their characteristics difference, it implies that their adaptability, litter size, growth rate, feed conversion, and the quality of meat they produce would also differ. Therefore, knowing and going after the rabbit breed appropriate for your farming needs and goals is essential to successful production.

   This chapter provides you with the different rabbit breeds suitable for meat production. You will discover the factors that make these rabbit breeds suitable, along with some popular meat breeds and their unique needs.

Various Rabbit Breeds Most Suitable for Meat Production

New Zealand White

New Zealand White is a known meat-producing breed.
https://commons.wikimedia.org/wiki/File:NewZealandWhiteRabbit_2.jpg

New Zealand White is a known meat-producing breed. It grows very fast, and its meat is tasty and soft. The amount of meat in a New Zealand White rabbit is more than its bone, and the meat flavor is excellent. The New Zealand White has a large litter size, that is, eight to twelve kits per litter on average, coupled with an exceptional feed conversion ratio and a rapid growth rate. These traits make the New Zealand White an effective breed suitable for meat production.

For adaptability, the New Zealand White can be reared in different climates, and they are very easy to look after. Additionally, you can easily manage them because they are compliant, which makes them a good option for anyone new to rabbit farming.

The New Zealand breed is certainly the breed for meat production due to its fast growth rate, yield, and overall management.

Californian

Another well-known breed for meat production, with a weight growth of eight to 12 pounds in 12 weeks, is the Californian. This breed is known for its tender and flavorful meat. It has an exceptional meat-to-bone ratio, which is sought after by restaurants and butchers.

Furthermore, the Californian grows rapidly, and its good conversion rate makes it an effective breed for producing meat. The average litter size of the Californian is six to eight per litter, and their growth rate is similar to that of the New Zealand White.

As for the ability to adapt, you can easily rear the Californian breed in any climate, and they are easy to nurture. The Californian breed has a gentle disposition. It is a crossbreed between the New Zealand Whites and the Chinchilla rabbits.

American Chinchilla

Due to the popularity of their meat and fur, this breed is called a dual-purpose rabbit. With a weight of over 12 pounds and a stocky body, they are regarded as one of the finest meat breed rabbits in the world. People favor this breed for its broad shoulder and superior deep loin, seen in various smoked and cooked dishes worldwide. Due to its popularity, this breed of rabbit is considered endangered.

American Chinchillas make good mothers and are known to give birth to eight to twelve kits. Additionally, they are very friendly, weigh between nine and 12 pounds, and have an exceptional meat-to-bone ratio.

Rex

Rex is considered a popular breed for meat production.
DestinationFearFan, CC BY-SA 4.0 <https://creativecommons.org/licenses/by-sa/4.0>, via Wikimedia Commons: https://commons.wikimedia.org/wiki/File:Rex_rabbit_(calico).jpg

Rex is also considered a popular breed for meat production. It weighs seven to 11 pounds and averages six to 12 kits per litter. This breed can be purchased easily in the US and is appreciated for its velvety pelt and meat-to-bone ratio. However, the Rex breed takes longer to get to the dinner table when compared with the New Zealand white.

Champagne D'Argent

The Champagne D'Argent breed is well-regarded around the world. This breed is known as the godfather of rabbits and has been a source of meat since 1631. Champagne D'Argent got its name from the city of Champagne in France, where it originated. A mature Champagne D'Argent has a weight of nine pounds with an uncommon amount of bone-to-meat. You can get both meat and fur from a Champagne D'Argent breed.

Silver Fox

The Silver Fox is known for its good meat quality and fur among small-scale farmers. Within three months, they can reach 10 to 12 pounds. They usually have medium-sized litters of between seven and eight kits. They are also rare, as they are considered an endangered breed. Individuals skilled in tanning hides highly prize the silver Fox breed's stunning pelt.

Satin Rabbits

The Satin breed is regarded as one of the heaviest and largest rabbit breeds, weighing over 12 pounds when fully grown. This rabbit produces a reasonable amount of meat due to its larger body size. Satins have a docile and calm temperament. They are the ideal breed of meat rabbits to nurture on your farm.

Cinnamon Rabbits

This breed is a cross between the New Zealand and American chinchilla rabbit. Although the initial purpose of this rabbit wasn't to produce meat, with its 11-pound weight when fully mature, it is certainly a breed to be considered for commercial purposes. The Cinnamon rabbit is red, prized for its fur, and can be kept as a pet. Nevertheless, this breed is hard to find.

Palomino Rabbit

Palomino rabbits have been known as meat rabbits for decades.
Jamaltby at en.Wikipedia, CC BY-SA 3.0 <https://creativecommons.org/licenses/by-sa/3.0>, via Wikimedia Commons: https://commons.wikimedia.org/wiki/File:PalBuckSide-small.jpg

This breed has been known as a meat rabbit for decades, popular for producing meat for both subsistence and commercial purposes. Palomino rabbits weigh 8 to 11 pounds when mature and have an excellent meat-to-bone ratio. The palomino rabbit has an easy-going temperament, which is why you can raise them. Nevertheless, you must be patient with them as their growth process is usually slow compared to other meat-producing rabbits.

American Blue

The American Blue rabbit can give you both meat and fur. It weighs nine to 12 pounds, and being an excellent mother, it averages 8 to 10 kits per litter. Sadly, it has a poor meat-to-bone rate like the Flemish Giant and is better off when crossbred with other breeds such as Silver Fox, Harlequin, Rex, or any other smaller breed.

Factors That Make a Rabbit Breed Suitable

There are certain factors to check for when choosing a suitable breed for meat production. These include growth rate, typical adult sizes, and overall temperaments.

Growth Rate

The growth rate of a breed is vital when considering a rabbit breed for your farm. This is key because a rapidly growing rabbit produces an early harvest, leading to regular meat production. When dealing with growth rates, consider quality breeding stock. Choose rabbits from thrifty lines that can quickly pay for themselves in feed savings alone. Seek out breeders with a good track record and purchase from them. Remember to look elsewhere if the breeder you are dealing with cannot tell you what their kits weigh at eight weeks.

Additionally, when choosing rabbits with a good growth rate, find rabbits with quality meat bloodlines. Good meat bloodlines are breeds of rabbits selected over generations for their meaty body type, rapid growth rate, and thriftiness. The offspring of these fast growers also tend to mimic these great qualities.

Furthermore, go for commercial rabbit breeds that have a fine bone structure. The offspring of these breeds are known to be speedy growers with an excellent meat-to-bone ratio, mainly from a 60 to 65 % dress-out rate. At maturity, adults weigh eight to twelve pounds.

Don't make the mistake of adding large-boned rabbits like Flemish Giants to your meat breeding program if you're looking for a faster growth rate. If you do, you will likely have a 5# fryer at eight weeks, which may not have much meat due to its large structure. Since rabbits grow bones before they grow meat, they may clean you out at five to six months old before they develop enough meat to account for their butchering. New Zealand and California breeds are well-known for commercial production because of their fast growth rate and litter size. On the other hand, heritage breeds are suitable for meat production in backyards and small farms.

Typical Adult Sizes

Most people commonly believe rabbits ought to be small pets. Due to this assumption, they are surprised when the baby rabbit they bring home turns into a giant rabbit the size of a cat! For example, the Holland Lop is a small breed of domestic rabbit, but many people find it big. Even "dwarf" and "mini" rabbit breed sizes may be considered big to some people, as they can become up to five pounds.

The Average Size of Adult Rabbits

Rabbits vary in size based on their breed and age. Therefore, while the average-sized adult house rabbit weighs six pounds, it doesn't help you to imagine the size your backyard meat rabbit will grow to. Some rabbits are large, while others are small; get the facts before you choose your breed.

• Small Rabbits

Small rabbits comprise mostly the mini and dwarf breed rabbits. The weight of these rabbits will never exceed five pounds. Surprisingly, this category has the fewest number of rabbit breeds. The American Rabbit Breeders Association (ARBA) recognizes 50 rabbit breeds, out of which only 11 are under the 5-pound category weight bracket.

These rabbits are considered house pets because they are bred for their small sizes.

Small rabbits comprise mostly the mini and dwarf breed rabbits.
https://pixabay.com/photos/rabbit-bunny-easter-grass-cute-4813172/

• Medium Rabbits

Most of the commonly known rabbits are in the medium category. The adult weight of these rabbits is around five to eight pounds. You will see most rabbits weigh around five or six pounds, which is lower when compared to the given range. Even though medium rabbits are smaller than other rabbit breeds, they have an average size of two to three times bigger than most people anticipate for a backyard rabbit. Fifteen breeds of rabbits fall into this category.

• Large Rabbits

Rabbits in the large category have a typical adult size of eight to 15 pounds! The majority of these larger breeds are fostered mainly as meat-producing rabbits. However, even though most ARBA-recognized breeds are large rabbits, they are difficult to come by.

How to Know the Typical Adult Size of Your Rabbit

If you have a baby rabbit and are eager to find out how big it will get, there are simple ways to estimate it. Knowing the estimated size will enable you to prepare enough space for when they reach their full adult size.

- **Consider Their Breed**

An effective way to estimate the typical adult size of your rabbit is to consider their breed. A rabbit breed chart online will guide you on the size range to expect from your rabbit if you already know their breed.

- **Consider Their Age**

If your rabbit was adopted and it is hard to tell the breed, you can still estimate their typical adult size based on their age. Knowing your rabbit's current age will be a pointer for their weight. These tips will give you a close estimate of what to expect from the expected adult size of your rabbit.

- When your rabbit is about four months old, it will probably be half its adult size. For instance, if your small rabbit is currently three pounds, it will grow to be around six pounds as an adult.

- Your rabbit will probably be ⅔ of its adult size when it is over six to eight months old. For example, your adopted rabbit is not a year old and certainly not a baby; they will grow up a little. If your rabbit is three pounds at this age, their adult size will most likely be around 4.5 pounds.

Overall Temperaments

There are many misconceptions about rabbits. The most common one is that rabbits like to be held and cuddled because of their plush toy look. On the contrary, rabbits become active and assert their personalities once they reach sexual maturity. When they reach that stage, some people get rid of them because of limited information on how to raise them.

Rabbits have wide-ranging personalities, even among their littermates. They can be high-spirited, shy, timid, curious, gentle, and silly, regardless of breed type or sex. They show affection by climbing on your back, nibbling at your socks, or sitting close to you. Some can even go as far as licking your face or hand. Even belligerent rabbits can become affectionate toward you when given room to bloom.

The act of neutering can eliminate many behavioral problems and diseases in rabbits. Compared to larger rabbits, smaller and dwarf rabbits are more active than their older counterparts. Due to their lightweight, they can jump higher than the larger ones. A neutered backyard rabbit has an eight to 10-year average lifespan, though it tends to exceed that.

During their adolescent stage, rabbits display behaviors such as biting, spraying, nest building, loss of house training, nipping, courtship behaviors, and destructiveness like circling and mounting. Exhibiting these behaviors is not a sign of something wrong with your rabbit; it is typical development behavior. Consult a specialized veterinarian to get them neutered.

Furthermore, biting is your rabbit's way of relaying messages like bossiness, irritation, fear, lust, and curiosity. With a nip, rabbits tell each other to get out of the way! Do not offer your hand to your rabbit as a greeting or playful gesture. Your rabbit could interpret that as an intrusion or a threat.

Popular Meat Breeds, Their Special Needs, and Considerations

• **New Zealand White**

Physical Characteristics

New Zealand white is the most popular among the diverse varieties of the New Zealand breeds. It has a pure white color with bright pink eyes. New Zealand Whites have round cheeks, muscular faces, and slender, well-rounded bodies. They have small, short pectoral muscles and large, long back feet. Its average body weight is up to 11 lb.

Housing

New Zealand whites are best kept indoors to protect them from extreme weather and predators. Do not house your rabbits in areas you rarely frequent, as rabbits are social animals and enjoy company. Use a pen that is four times the length of your rabbit when it stretches. To give your rabbit a larger space, use dog playpens, which are bigger compared to commercial rabbit cages that are insufficient to house your rabbits. For at least five hours a day, give your rabbits the liberty to leave their cage. It will enable them to remain in a room without a pen or wander freely in your house.

See to it that the space allotted to your rabbits is rabbit-proofed! New Zealand whites have a natural tendency to chew and dig their way out, which can damage property like curtains, cords, rugs, furniture, and carpet. Also, make sure electrical wires are out of their reach.

Feeding

New Zealand Whites need a lot of fresh hay and water. Use hays like Timothy hay or other mixed grass hays. Every day, ensure you give your rabbit fresh, leafy vegetables. Supply at least one-fourth cup of vegetables for every pound of body weight. Some of the vegetables that a New Zealand White rabbit needs include carrot tops, bok choy red lettuce, and dandelion green.

Furthermore, you can use herbs like parsley, mint, cilantro, and basil to feed your rabbit. Non-leafy vegetables are considered unsafe for your rabbit, so abstain from feeding them. Feed your New Zealand White rabbits less carrots because of their high sugar level. Consult your veterinarian if you are unsure what food to give your rabbits.

Furthermore, you can use pellets from the store to complement your New Zealand Whites' diet. A timothy pellet with an 18% fiber content would suffice for an adult rabbit. However, the pellets should form a small amount of their diet, and you should never exceed the amount shown on the pellet's package.

Small amounts of fruit like pears, berries, melon, and apples can be given to your rabbit—one tablespoon for every three pounds of body weight.

Breeding

Breeding New Zealand Whites is simple. A doe becomes fertile between 8 and 12 weeks of age and can be bred at five to eight months. They are fertile throughout the year and have a gestation period of 28 to 35 days. However, most births take place at 31 to 32 days.

Care

Nurturing your rabbits will keep them healthy and encourage them to be productive.

Uses

The New Zealand White's primary use is meat production. They are fast growers, with their offspring (fryers) slaughtered at two months old. Their fur is used to make fur trimmings in the fashion industry. Apart from their meat and fur production, the New Zealand White is used for commercial rabbit farming and for raising as pets.

Personality

New Zealand White breeds are outgoing and calm. They live well with both humans and other rabbits, making them social. They are a good option as pets because they can be handled easier than smaller breeds. Ensure you watch when children and other pets are close to your rabbits. Sudden movements and loud noises stress them easily. When they are not neutered, they act in a territorial manner.

- **Californian Rabbits**

Californian rabbits are reared for either their fur or their meat and are suitable as pets.
https://commons.wikimedia.org/wiki/File:Californian_Rabbit.JPG

Californian rabbits are among the most commercially bred rabbits in the US. They are often reared for either their fur or their meat and are suitable as pets.

Physical Characteristics

The Californian breed has a well-rounded, compact body and is large.

The Californian rabbit is similar in color to the Himalayan, having colored points with a white body. Its ears are big and stand erect. A brown marking is found on their tail, feet, ears, and nose. Californian rabbits have pink eyes and very short necks. They have full shoulders and are very muscular. They also have a silky and soft coat.

The Californian adult weighs 12 lb. on average.

Housing

Californian rabbits can either live in the house or outside the house. When going for a cage, ensure it's wide and long, with enough space for hopping and jumping. It will keep them healthier and happier.

It's normal for rabbits to chew their cage. This is why it is wise to ensure that the cage materials cannot easily be broken by your rabbit. A cage with a metal frame, a plastic bottom, or a metal bar with wire enclosing the sides can be cleaned easily and will keep the rabbit from destroying your home. If your cage is an all-wire design, ensure there is a resting place for your rabbit to avoid hurting its feet when sitting on the wire base. A nesting area built into the cage would do the trick, as it would help the rabbits avoid contact with the cage's base.

Feeding

Californian rabbits require a diet of vitamins A, D, and E and fiber. They need enough fat and protein. Pregnant or nursing females and growing rabbits need more protein than mature rabbits.

You can feed your rabbits fresh water, plenty of timothy hay, and a little pellet feed to give them the required nutrients. A matured Californian rabbit needs half a cup of pellets daily.

Feed your rabbits a lot of leafy vegetables with small amounts of carbohydrates. Some food items you can use include Radicchio, apples, pear, kale, green peppers, berries, broccoli, bok choy, etc.

Refrain from feeding your Californian rabbits food high in calories, seeds or nuts, grains, cookies, and bread. If you must give your rabbit carrots, do so in small amounts, as too many carrots can cause them harm.

Breeding

Californian rabbits can breed without human support. This rabbit has a gestation period of 28 to 31 days. A doe can give birth to two to eight kits at a time.

Care

Taking care of your rabbit is vital, especially if you are into commercial rabbit farming. Ensure that the pregnant nursing mother and breeding male are healthy. Regularly check them and always seek the services of a good vet while caring for them.

Uses

Californian rabbits are used for both their fur value and for meat production. It's an excellent breed to go for when going into commercial rabbit production. Furthermore, you can either raise them as show rabbits or pets.

Personality

Californian rabbits have a docile personality and can easily be managed.

- ## Flemish Giant

The Flemish Giant is the world's largest breed and one of the oldest. This breed is adaptable, gentle, and reared for its meat and fur.

Physical Characteristics

Apart from being one of the largest breeds in the world, their bodies are long with a broad back and solid, fleshed, well-rounded hindquarters. Although strong and muscular, their legs are of average length. Their ears are large and positioned in a V shape above their head. The head of the male Flemish Giant is broader and more imposing than that of the female.

Flemish Giants have a dense undercoat and smooth, medium-length hair with a glossy sheen. They exist in many varieties around the world. According to ARBA, there are seven color varieties: White, Sandy, Light Gray, Steel Gray, Fawn, Black, and Blue.

Flemish Giants have a body weight of up to 22 lb. However, the minimum standard weight for a senior buck is around 13 lb., while a senior doe is about 14 lb.

Housing

Due to their size, design a bigger cage with a larger enclosure. The minimum size for their cage is 3 x 4 feet. Smaller cages would cause them to be stressed because of their size.

Feeding

Since they don't overeat, feeding them with special commercialized pellets should do. Additionally, you can feed them cabbage, carrots, potatoes, parsley, pineapple, strawberries, corn, etc. Introduce these foods one at a time until their digestive system is accustomed to them.

For every five pounds of weight, Flemish Giants should be given two to four cups of vegetables daily. Put fresh water in their cage daily.

Breeding

Eight-month-old female Flemish giants are old enough to give birth after the 31st day. Its litter size averages 5 to 12 per litter. Since they are an old breed of domesticated rabbit, Flemish giants find it hard to breed with wild rabbits because of differences in their respective chromosomes.

Care

Flemish giants are gentle, obedient, and can adapt to any home. Although they can be considered pets, caution should be taken when kids are around them because they bite when they feel threatened or upset.

Uses

The Flemish Giant rabbit is well-known as a pet. Furthermore, they are suitable for producing meat and fur. This breed is also a popular show animal.

Personality

Though their looks and large size can throw you off, they are gentle giants. They love attention and are very friendly. They are peaceful creatures and crave a peaceful life. This doesn't mean you can push them around. They may scratch or bite you if you mistreat them.

Though daunting, choosing the right breed of rabbits for meat production is a wonderful experience. You now know the right breeds for meat production and how to get the best out of them. Enjoy your journey into raising the world's next source of meat.

Chapter 3: Creating a Healthy Environment

Rabbits are fragile yet active animals. They need to be kept healthy and comfortable. If you're new to rabbit farming, then there are terms you'll need to know. First, rabbit farming can also be called "cuniculture." Cuniculture allows you to breed domestic rabbits as a source of meat, fur, or both. To successfully raise these livestock, you must create a healthy and safe space where they can feed, breathe, nest, and breed. Rearing rabbits is an uncomplicated business that requires very few materials and resources. Rabbits eat almost anything nutritious. So, if you're excited and enthusiastic about starting this fruitful journey, this chapter provides the steps to follow.

You'll discover the secret behind raising your rabbits and doing it brilliantly. You'll also discover the space needed for a start-up, the suitable materials, and the best location for breeding, and learn how to create and maintain a hygienic environment. Apart from these elements, other factors, such as protecting your rabbits from predators and diseases, will also be discussed.

What Do Rabbits Need for a Comfortable Home?

Rabbits need enough room for a hop, jump, or run. They can get very active, so you need to make room for digging, as well as protection from predators and extreme weather changes. The space needs to be well-ventilated, thoroughly dry, and damp-free. A dirty environment causes illness and uneasiness. The height of that space also needs to be considered. You don't want their ears or heads touching the roof when they stand upright. You can use specific materials to build an effective shielded and cool area for them. Rabbits need a place to hide if they sense the presence of prey, for example, snakes, dogs, foxes, woodpeckers, and cats.

Rabbits need enough room for a hop, jump, or run.
https://unsplash.com/photos/ygqaLPkaB2o

For this purpose, you create some cozy holes in the rabbit room where they can escape when frightened. Rabbits can easily get bored and suffer when left in the same place for too long. This requires you to give them regular exercise. You may wonder what this consists of. Just let them out of their rooms into a protected space where they can hop and jump freely. One other vital element is the bed area. Rabbits can easily adapt to a cold temperature, but that may take time if they have never been exposed to it before. In the meantime, provide dust-free hay or straw, which is also safe to eat if they decide to take a snack at any time.

Selecting the Appropriate Hutch Materials

A hutch is a nesting area built specifically for raising rabbits. As a rabbit farmer, selecting suitable materials for building a hutch helps promote a healthy environment for your rabbit's growth. There are many elements for the perfect space, size, and design for raising your rabbits.

Hutch Size

Your hutch needs to be as big as possible. The minimum size for a rabbit breeding area should be no less than 12 square feet. You can add additional space for exercise purposes. The hutch should be designed so that the bed and exercise spaces are built together in one location so you don't have to move them to rest, feed, exercise, or excrete. As for the minimum spacing of a rabbit room, ensure that it is three to four times the size of the rabbit. You also need to consider the number of rabbits you'll be housing.

The greater the number, the larger the space needed. So, think upscale and future enlargement when planning.

Hutch Location

The hutch can be either indoors or outdoors. Look around your home and find unused cupboard areas or alcoves to transform into rabbit housing. Make sure you calculate the maximum number of rabbits likely to be contained in the housing being planned.

Design Materials

You must look for chewable and non-toxic materials when building your rabbit housing. Rabbits like to get busy, especially with their mouths, so you want to ensure that any materials found within their reach should at least be chewable without causing harm to them. There are so many options you can look out for when considering a decent house for your bunnies.

- **Woods**: Try out pine or plywood, which are common and preferable for outdoor housing. Even when ingested, they are harmless compared to an MDF, which is toxic. There are other textures of wood you can use. For example, trim can be used as a good cover for the edges of the house, which are likely to get chewed by the bunnies. For example, try a skirting board.

- **Plastics**: Plastics can hardly be avoided. A great blend would be using Correx, but it is not chewable. If you're still at the beginning of construction, using little or no plastic for housing is much preferable as, when broken, it can become sharp.

- **A Mesh of Wires**: To add to the aesthetics, you should add mesh. Mesh does not entirely need to be made of wire; you can finish up with something as simple as chicken wire or, preferably, a mesh coated with powder, plastic, or plastikote. The latter are non-toxic when dried, come in different colors and look good. You can place it within the frame of doors and windows for a better fit to prevent chewing.

• **The Flooring**: Choosing the appropriate flooring that makes it easy for you to clean is your best option. Hard flooring is a much better option, for example, safety flooring or lino. They are both cheap and easy to install. A safety flooring is way harder in texture than a standard lino. You mostly find them in a vet's waiting room. To fit it, apply a flooring adhesive or a double-sided tape and lay it on top. To complete, you can apply a sealant around the edges to create the perfect finishing touches. Tiles are good options as well. The only catch would be that you'll need to avoid shiny and slippery tiles so your rabbits find it easy to move around. These floors should be easy to clean.

Determining Adequate Spacing for Each Rabbit

You can plan many elements to include in your rabbit enclosure, but it's easy to overlook space planning. It's easy when planning for one rabbit, but deciding on more isn't always that easy. You may under-calculate the space and end up packing the poor bunnies into a space that is too small. The minimum spacing required for a rabbit is dependent on many factors:

• Breed types
• Size of rabbit
• Weight of rabbit

You calculate the cage size by multiplying the length and width of the cage. Remember that all amenities inside the cage, including the water basin and food tray, must be subtracted from the result. When you provide the appropriate house space for your rabbits, you're guaranteed that they will grow and develop healthily.

How Much House Spacing Do Rabbits Need?

The home should be comfortable and easy to move around. However, rabbits' sizes vary, which should be considered when planning the housing size. They also vary in weight. For example, the Netherland dwarfs weigh just two pounds compared to the Flemish giant of 15 pounds. Make sure you take this factor into account. If your rabbit is still in its early growth stage, you will need to adjust your calculations for its possible adult size. If you're unsure of the eventual size, you can wait it out before opting for an enclosure expansion.

- **Minimum Hutch Length**

The best and easiest way to determine the hop length of your rabbit is by taking a measurement starting from their nose to toe when they are stretched out, then multiplying this length by three. This will give you the minimum enclosure length. For example, say you measure a small-sized three-pound rabbit while it was lying across the floor to be 12 inches long; 12 inches multiplied by three would give you 36 inches. This results in a 3-4 feet length enclosure, which should be the minimum. It should never be smaller than this because the rabbit only grows bigger and longer. They will feel cramped if you do not expand the enclosure with time.

- **Minimum Hutch Height**

As much as your rabbit's house length needs some calculating, so does the height. You don't want to create a compartment where they could end up hurting their heads when they hop. When there isn't enough room for them to stand on their feet, they can develop a spinal deformity. The worst case is that they may lose their spinal flexibility, a far greater risk for them. Giving your rabbits at least 2-3 feet of vertical spacing is as vital as horizontal spacing.

- **Minimum Width**

The width needs to be just as wide as the length, even more, to prevent any cramped conditions. To measure, you'll need to add a few more inches to your rabbit's already measured length, given from previous examples. Here's another example of how to apply this. Assuming the length of your rabbit is 14 inches or 16 inches at most, you would need to provide enough wiggle room that should be about 4×2 feet, which results in eight square feet for your rabbit.

Giving Your Rabbits Sufficient Space to Multiply

Are you thinking of increasing the population of your bunnies? Then, you'll need to put some more elements in place, like more bed space, food supply, and more room for exercise. Thinking about more spacing may seem overwhelming, but you'll have to start somewhere. For example, the space increment can depend on the size and weight of your rabbits. That's why having a playpen is a better bet, as it would save you the stress of immediate expansion of housing. A playpen can hold two bunnies with very low weight and size compared to bigger and heavier breeds. In this case, you need an expansion as quickly as possible. Rabbits grow within the blink of an eye.

Rabbits grow within the blink of an eye.
https://unsplash.com/photos/J_cqfq9FjmU

There isn't a specific guideline for knowing the right timing or calculation to expand your housing, but it's vital to understand that each female rabbit can give birth to four to eight little bunnies. When it eventually gets to this state, you might have to vacate your family room so they can all feel at home and happy. The next question would be, "How Can I Eventually Expand the Housing?" To begin, you must have a small enclosure sufficient for at least a rabbit. Then, you can start to expand the enclosures. If you did not have a rabbit house before, then it's even easier for you. All you'll have to do is follow the guidelines above. This will give you the perfect square feet for a healthy space. If this is not the case for you, don't worry. You can still expand spacing to give you your desired result. Here's how:

- **Expand Enclosure:** First, you must expand the size of your enclosure. To do this, you can attach other compartments, for example, an exercise pen. You can try this out even without completely replacing their home.

- **Utilize Spaces under Furniture**: If you live in a tiny home or apartment, you can use the space underneath your furniture for the rabbit's enclosure, creating more vertical spacing to compensate for the small length of the area. A good example of furniture to utilize would be under your dining table.

- **More Vertical Space**: If your rabbits are likely to hop and jump around frequently, then it would be wise to create more vertical platforms to give them more room to move around.
- **Roaming about Freely**: You won't need to contain your rabbit for longer if you feel they're sufficiently trained. You can seal off every exit to prevent escape and let them move around a bit.

Creating Space for Feeding, Nesting, and Waste Management

A rabbit's home is its environment. This is much more than where it eats, sleeps, or exercises. Wherever and whatever it can access can be classified as a homely environment. As mentioned earlier, this also contains the necessary amenities for its survival, including bedding, trays for food, hay, or straw. There should be adequate ventilation and protection from predators. A suitable resting rabbit home should contain at least 50% of the following:

- Undisturbed food and water.
- A place for resting and comfort.
- A place to exercise and explore safely.
- A place to hide when frightened.
- A space to chew whatever and whenever.
- A place to escape to interact with companions.
- A place for shelter from any change in temperature.

A rabbit's resting area could be expanded to different segments. As mentioned earlier, one would be a dark-covered room for sleeping away from the noise and the other for eating and relaxing. All spaces should be drought and free of dampness to avoid poor ventilation.

Housing and Waste Management

What is a suitable toilet area for your rabbits? Rabbits need access to a regular toilet site. For this purpose, you can provide trays lined with straw, hay, or newspapers. A rabbit's mouth is constantly busy with food, so you can be rest assured that they will pass a lot of waste. Ensure that the toilet area is separate from the sleeping area. Hay and trays used in the toilet areas must not be made of toxic material. In addition, making good use of wire for housing is essential, and applying solid flooring for easy and regular clean-up.

The bedding area should come with an extra insulator for extra cold weather. It is not advisable to use wood shelving as a bedding material, and the exercise area cannot be overlooked. There are still elements that need to be mentioned. For example:

- Rabbits should have access to a place to run daily.
- The exercise area must contain raised spaces for jumping. This room should be outdoors.
- It should be secured enough to prevent any entry of predators.
- If possible, it can be moved from time to time to avoid burrowing or overgrazing.
- Provide a covering or shade for windy or rainy days.
- There should be enough room for all the rabbits to be together or alone in one place.

Tips and Strategies for Maintaining the Hutch

Cleanliness

Hygiene is necessary for the health of your rabbits. You want to maintain the state and environment in which they live to prevent illness or disease. Here are a few factors to help:

- The rabbit sleeping area should be thoroughly cleaned on a daily basis. To do this, remove wet or dirty shelving or bed areas and take out spoilt or old food.
- The entire living area, indoors and outdoors, should be cleaned at least once every week. This must be done to maintain a clean, hygienic environment for your rabbits.

- Use mild pet-friendly disinfectant if possible. Just like a rabbit is fragile physically, their immunity is just as fragile.

Temperature Regulation

- Most healthy rabbits get acclimatized to an outdoor environment. They can withstand any temperature difference as long as they are provided with good nutritional food and housing.

- Those rabbits accustomed to indoor housing should not be suddenly placed outside in cold weather. If you want your bunny to stay alive during winter, you must gradually expose them to the indoors beforehand.
- Old or very young rabbits should never be allowed outside because they cannot tolerate vast temperature differences all at once.
- Certain temperatures are still considered too much for even a healthy adult rabbit, for example, 20 degrees Fahrenheit.

Creating a proper and healthy living environment for your bunnies requires study and measurements. If you want to raise a hutch of bunnies for domestic purposes, you must put certain factors into place. Rabbit farming can be fruitful enough to provide a profitable and resourceful income for a farmer. It is also a good source of quality protein meat. The art of raising rabbits for meat is known as Cuniculture, and to begin farming, you need a good location with a good grazing source, preferably far from a residential area but close enough to a commercial setting. You don't have to start on a large scale. You can begin small and gradually build your numbers from there.

Choose a location with adequate transportation close by. Apart from this, your rabbits must be in good health, so creating enough room for growth and exercise, where temperature change can easily be regulated, is necessary. With all this in place, you are well on your way to a profitable rabbit farming business.

Chapter 4: Understanding Your Rabbits' Nutritional Needs

If you've gone down the rabbit hole of looking for the perfect rabbit meal plan, you're now probably confused and a little lost, too. Some people claim that vegetables and greens are all rabbits need to survive, while others advise against feeding rabbits too much of the green stuff. Then there are the people who swear by pellet feedings and consider pellets to be the only answer to rabbit sustenance. Hay is also considered a suitable food source for your rabbits. All these opinions and options are enough to make anyone feel confused.

In the midst of this nutritional overload, you find yourself playing the role of a rabbit diet detective, carefully calculating the perfect balance of greens, pellets, and hay. However, the thing is, there's no perfect meal plan that suits the needs of every bunny, though there is a general selection of nutritional foods you can follow. Although each bunny has its own preferences, some diet options are preferred over others for meat rabbits.

Types of Feed for Rabbits

When you're thinking about what to feed your rabbits, it's a good idea to consider your expertise. Suppose you're not an expert in nutrition, or you don't want to dive into the intricacies of ration formulation. In that case, there's a simple route to take. Start off with commercial rabbit pellets, as they're a reliable standard meal. As you get more comfortable, you can try the other feeding options. Remember, when it comes to feeding your rabbits, doing your homework is a must. Don't assume that because wild rabbits munch on grass, your meat rabbits can survive on the same menu. Don't just feed them anything because some vegetables can be *very toxic* for them.

On the other hand, the cost of rabbit food keeps climbing (and there's no sign of it slowing down anytime soon), which may make the idea of growing your own rabbit food sound appealing. However, only try this if you can be consistent with the process. Otherwise, it's all just a whole lot of waste.

Although each bunny has its own preferences, some diet options are preferred over others for meat rabbits.

1. Pellets

If you're looking for a quick, easy, and well-balanced option, go for good-quality organic or non-organic pellets, as they're a safe bet. If you've ever thought about making your own rabbit food from scratch, be warned that it's not as straightforward as it may seem, given all the different factors you need to consider. If you're after an uncomplicated route, pellets are the solution. Eventually, you can gradually introduce fresh foods into the mix. In this way, you could even save some money by blending pellets with weeds or adding extra greens from your garden. If you want to rear your bunnies on a primarily fresh greens diet, then make sure the breed you choose can handle this kind of diet. Alternatively, you could connect with someone who's already raising rabbits and loves their leafy meals.

Pellets are like a rabbit's dream meal because they're perfectly formulated and balanced to meet all their nutritional needs. It's a tailor-made feast of essential vitamins and minerals, all designed to keep rabbits healthy and happy.

Alternatives to Pelleted Feed

You can also feed rabbits with what you grow in your garden or gather from the pasture. The joy of knowing you're providing something entirely homegrown can be very satisfying. However, it's essential to make sure your rabbits get a well-rounded diet for their well-being. Given the growing fascination with steering clear of pellet feeds and the move toward choosing natural, homegrown foods for your meat rabbits, here are some feed alternatives suitable for them:

1. Hay

Rabbits need high fiber for most of their diet. This can be met by feeding them hay. The basic ingredient of their meals should be quality grass hay. Look for hay that's clean, free of dust and mold, and which has enough protein to keep their systems working smoothly. Grass hay is the best choice. It's packed with fiber, which does wonders for their digestion. Make sure you avoid straight alfalfa hay, though many people think otherwise. For instance, alfalfa isn't grass; it's a legume that's fed to animals to increase their protein intake. Although plant protein is considered good for rabbits, alfalfa contains excessive calcium, which isn't favorable for your rabbits. In fact, it can result in concentrated urine, which leads to kidney stones, which is something you want to avoid under any circumstances. You can also try some other hay options, like Timothy grass or high-quality horse hay. If you wish to use alfalfa, you can combine it with grass to balance the nutrients. Oat grass is a good option for this, which can be easily found at horse feed supply stores.

2. Greens

Most cartoons show rabbits eating carrots and other vegetables, but did you know that a lot of these greens are not good for your rabbits? In fact, there are some greens you should steer clear of. For instance, Iceberg lettuce, although rabbits love to eat it, is, in fact, toxic for them. It's too watery and can lead to upset tummies and messy stools. Instead, go for dark and leafy greens like kale and leaf lettuce. These are bursting with vitamin A and other nutrients. A tip to remember is that once greens start looking old, they can become a fermenting mess. Stick to the fresh ones and offer only what your bunny can finish in around 15 minutes. Other greens that are suitable for your rabbits include radish greens, sunflower leaves, beet greens and roots, carrot tops, dill, mint, comfrey, and more. These are the greens your rabbits can happily eat.

3. Treat Foods

Treats like carrots, fruit, and starchy foods are packed with sugar. You should always give these treats in very small amounts. Why the caution? Well, the high sugar levels can really mess with your rabbit's gut health and cause digestive problems.

4. Rabbit Food Caveats

You should know that wild rabbits can munch on almost anything. However, your pet rabbits, or even rabbits grown for meat, cannot do the same. They belong to different species. While they do have some common dietary preferences, they don't necessarily eat the same things. When wild rabbits are out and about, they nibble on fresh forage right where it grows. But it's not the same when it comes to your domestic rabbits. Dumping a bunch of restaurant veggie scraps into their pens is not a good idea. Even though your rabbit is an herbivore, this is a move you'll come to regret. Firstly, they won't get the proper nutrition, and secondly, those scraps will end up wilting and fermenting on the pen floor, drawing flies and causing a mess. And those yard clippings you had planned to give them are too delicate and will have already started wilting by the time they reach your bunny's bowl. Remember, what works for wild rabbits isn't always fit for their domestic counterparts.

5. Alfalfa Hay and Rolled Oats

A simple alternative feed idea is to use a mix of alfalfa hay and rolled oats. Rabbits usually love this combination and prefer it over regular hay. However, as already discussed, alfalfa hay has a considerable amount of protein and calcium. So, if you decide to go the alfalfa route, you've got to team it up with rolled oats so that your rabbits get some extra phosphorus, which helps balance out the high calcium levels from the alfalfa.

6. Oats and/or Barley

Consider oats and/or barley as a solid option. They work wonders, especially for those growing kits who are just starting to explore the world of food beyond milk. For the little ones who've recently weaned, these grains are gentle on their tummies and easy to digest. A good option is to keep a separate bowl of oats right inside the cage for the young ones. When choosing the oats and barley categories, opt for the uncut and unrolled options, as they're the best suited for beginners.

7. Black Oil Sunflower Seeds

You'll find these seeds in the bird feed section, and although they're typically used to feed birds, they work like magic on rabbit coats, too. If you're looking to give your rabbits a stunning appearance, consider giving them about a teaspoon of BOSS every day.

8. Alfalfa or Hay Cubes

Instead of giving your rabbits rough hay, try hay cubes. These neat little compressed blocks are made from alfalfa or hay. They're not just plain cubes; they're also infused with molasses and packed tightly. They're like a chewy treat your rabbits can gnaw on, and that's important because rabbits' teeth never stop growing. You can find bags of these cubes in a rabbit feed store, or if you prefer the bigger ones, you can always head over to the horse feed store or section. The latter actually provide better value and are also helpful for your rabbit's dental health.

9. Calf Manna

This is something that stands out from the crowd. Calf Manna is not just a name; it's a brand of supplement that works wonders. This is specially crafted to boost milk production in a variety of animals. If you have a pregnant or nursing rabbit, giving her a couple of teaspoons of Calf Manna each day can make a big difference. It's especially good for meat-breed rabbits that tend to have quite sizable litter. By ensuring your mama rabbit gets her Calf Manna, you're helping her provide enough milk for her kits and ensuring she stays in tip-top shape throughout pregnancy and nursing. This smart move could even allow you to breed her sooner for another round of kits.

10. Dried or Fresh Fruit

Both dried and fresh varieties of fruit are great for rabbits. These colorful treats can add a little excitement to your rabbit's diet. However, while they're a nice occasional treat, it's important not to overdo it. In addition, many of these fruits deal with specific problems. For example, pineapples can actually help if your rabbit suffers from a bout of "fur block." This happens when rabbits ingest too much of their own fur, causing a blockage in their digestive system. And then there's papaya – not only is it tasty, but it can also serve a practical purpose. If you notice your rabbit's urine has a strong odor, papaya can help reduce that.

11. Weeds, Lawn Trimmings, and Bush Trimmings

Some natural feed for your rabbits includes weeds, lawn trimmings, and bush clippings. These can actually be pretty useful for your rabbits. Greens not only include the vegetables you can feed your rabbits but also grass, weeds, lawn trimmings, and even leaves. Just be sure they're on the safe-to-eat list. Some of the good wild plant choices are comfrey, chickweed, cow parsley, docks, cattails, dandelion, plantain, shepherd's purse, sow thistle, and watercress. You might want to refer to a safe list online.

Dandelions are like rabbit candy – they love them so much that you may just become a dandelion farmer in your own yard. Freshly cut grass is another winner in their eyes. Many people set up a little rabbit play area with wire fencing or use a dog crate to let their bunnies roam and nibble on these natural goodies while they tidy up their living spaces. It's a win-win situation, but be extra careful to make sure there are no toxic weeds within reach.

Nutrient Breakdown

Your rabbit's diet should have a combination of nutrients to ensure they can grow most effectively.

• Carbohydrates

Think of these as energy boosters. Rabbits can balance their own diet – they'll munch more if their energy level is low and less if it's high, but too much energy (read: carbs) can actually slow down their digestion. So, tread carefully and find the right balance.

• Fiber

Fiber is a rabbit's best friend. Wild rabbits eat loads of it, and while young bunnies need a bit less, it's still super important. When feeding your adult rabbits, it's best to have at least 25% fiber in their food. So, look for the ones with the highest fiber content.

• Minerals

The rabbit food discussed above usually contains all the minerals required for a healthy diet except for cobalt. It is the missing component that you have to fill some other way.

- **Vitamins**

Your rabbits have some friendly bacteria in their intestines - vitamin B-complex and vitamin C, which also means they need to get vitamins A, D, and E from their diet. So, make sure these vitamins are included in their pellet mix.

Keep in mind that moderation is key. Don't go overboard with food. Feed your rabbits about twice a day to keep their intake balanced. However, stay clear of fermented and sour foods, as they can create problems. If you prefer to use pellet food for your bunnies, keep an eye on their weight because they can gain too much too fast, which is something you'll want to avoid.

Balancing the Diet

Rabbits have unique dietary needs, and getting the right balance of nutrients is vital to keeping them flourishing. The best way to achieve this is to combine all the different food sources. You can start with commercially produced rabbit feed, i.e., pellets. These specially formulated feeds are a nutritional goldmine designed to meet your rabbits' dietary requirements. While the idea of crafting your own mix is tempting, it's a bit of a nutritional tightrope, and finding that perfect balance can be challenging. So, leaning on the expertise of commercial feeds is a smart choice.

Rabbits have unique dietary needs, and getting the right balance of nutrients is key to keeping them flourishing.

https://www.pexels.com/photo/fruit-slices-balancing-on-a-line-7465042/

Next, there's protein – a key player in your rabbit's diet. Commercial feeds usually offer protein levels ranging from 14 to 18 percent. For rabbits raised with a focus on meat production, a diet rich in protein (around 16 to 18 percent) can be a growth accelerator. Keep your feed cool and dry to prevent unwanted mold growth. The airflow should be suitable, and make sure not to leave the feed open and accessible to sneaky rodents. Keep it protected in chew-proof containers.

In addition, you should incorporate hay into your rabbit's diet, as it not only supplements their diet but also keeps them engaged and helps maintain their dental health. There's a variety of hay types to choose from; your choice of hay should align with your rabbits' dietary needs. For example, if you're providing lower-protein pellets, consider balancing it out with high-protein alfalfa hay.

Feeding Guidelines

The amount of food your rabbits need isn't a one-size-fits-all deal. Each rabbit has different nutritional needs, especially when characterized as young or adult. It also depends on the rabbit's living conditions and how much food they should be given. For instance, when the weather turns cold, they need a bit more food, whereas in the summer, they can be given less.

You can also decide how much food to give to your rabbits by keeping an eye on their weight. If they look too lean, they need more food, and vice versa. It's wise to keep a watchful eye on their portions when it comes to full-grown bucks that aren't currently breeding. The goal is to avoid pudgy rabbits – too much fluffiness can mess with their fertility and turn them into couch potatoes. On average, adult rabbits munch about four ounces of food per day. If you have rabbits with little ones, they'll need about eight ounces to keep up with the parenting hustle.

For those meaty breeds, the food scoop ranges from 1/2 to 1 cup daily – but it varies from rabbit to rabbit, just like your own food preferences. Now, here's where the debate comes in. Pregnant or nursing rabbits and growing kits may enjoy the luxury of free-feeding, and breeders will either nod in agreement or share raised eyebrows. More protein often translates to speedier growth and bigger bunnies, but the free-feeding question is a balancing act.

What to Do if a Rabbit Is off Their Feed

When your rabbit's appetite takes a detour, your first instinct may be to offer up some familiar treats or greens they've enjoyed in the past. It seems like a quick fix to get them nibbling again. However, these treats can sometimes fuel the fire, stirring up trouble in their digestive system and leading to loose stools. Instead, you should use a different approach. Offer a helping of good, clean grass hay, as it's like a soothing balm for their upset tummies. Another option on the menu is rolled oats, a high-fiber choice that's gentle on the digestive tract and a treat for their taste buds.

Speaking of essentials, don't forget the water supply. Rabbits need fresh, clean water. Give the water bottle or water line a quick glance to clear any blockages. Rabbits can get a bit finicky, and they're not ones to wait around for a drink. Without water, they can quickly dehydrate, and that's not good for their appetite. If your rabbit still isn't eating, check their droppings. If things are looking a bit runny, their diet needs more high-fiber food.

In conclusion, the diet of a rabbit controls many things, especially when you're growing them for meat. This dietary balance isn't just about filling bellies. It's a requirement for their growth and their ability to breed. Think of it as a delicate balance where the right mix of nutrients fuels their development, ensuring those young kits reach their full potential. And it's not just about the physical gains. The rabbit's diet can influence their behavior, energy levels, and even their reproductive abilities. Keep in mind that whenever you're tinkering with your rabbits' menu, take it slowly. Quick changes can spell trouble, and you definitely don't want that. Remember to give them plenty of water - not just a sip – as they need plenty of it.

Chapter 5: Preventing and Addressing Health Issues

Rabbits can develop health issues, diseases, and disorders just as easily as any other animal. When raising rabbits for meat, taking care that your bevy of bunnies is healthy and thriving is part of the deal. Knowing about common diseases and disorders can make it easier to address these health issues and prevent recurrences. This chapter provides an overview of the common diseases rabbits can develop, guidelines for prevention, treatment protocols, and everything else you need to know to keep rabbits healthy.

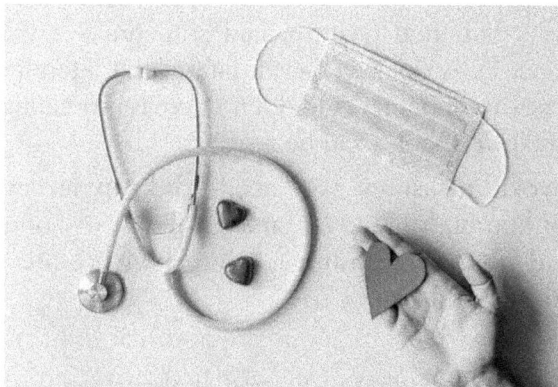

When raising rabbits for meat, taking care that your bevy of bunnies is healthy and thriving is part of the deal.

https://www.pexels.com/photo/medical-stethoscope-and-mask-composed-with-red-foiled-chocolate-hearts-4386466/

Common Health Issues Rabbits Face

A rabbit can live and reproduce for at least eight years when fed and cared for properly. However, there are several common diseases that rabbits can develop as they age. Here are some common conditions you need to be familiar with.

Respiratory Tract Infections

Unlike humans, a rabbit can only breathe through their noses. As the nose is the only orifice in rabbits for breathing, air-borne microorganisms and harmful chemicals can easily get in and infect the respiratory system. Although they have an immune system that can ward off harmful organisms and break down toxic chemicals, severe or prolonged exposure can eventually lead to an infection.

Rabbits with respiratory illnesses will sneeze repeatedly, and their breathing will be labored. These signs are associated with upper respiratory infections. Lower respiratory infections also occur where an added wheezing sound can be heard when you listen up close.

GI Stasis (Gastrointestinal Stasis)

GI stasis occurs when a rabbit's digestive system stops working or slows down, disrupting the normal movement of food and waste through the gut. This can be caused by a diet low in fiber, dehydration, stress, or other underlying health issues. Without proper food movement, the gut becomes compacted and leads to painful gas buildup, bloating, and discomfort. Symptoms include reduced appetite, smaller or no fecal pellets, lethargy, a hunched posture, and sometimes a visibly distended belly. GI stasis can be serious and even fatal if not attended to promptly. Watch for changes in appetite. A sudden decrease in eating or reluctance to eat hay and fresh vegetables can be a sign.

The two pivotal measures you need to keep an eye on include monitoring fecal output, looking for smaller, fewer, or abnormally shaped fecal pellets, and observing posture. A hunched posture or sitting in a stretched-out position is a sign of GI.

Dental Problems

Rabbits' teeth grow continuously, and if they become misaligned or overgrown, it can lead to various dental issues. Overgrown teeth can cause pain, injury to the cheeks and tongue, difficulty eating, and weight loss. Dental spurs, sharp points that develop on the teeth, can also cause discomfort. These problems often stem from genetics or an improper diet lacking sufficient fiber to wear down the teeth naturally. If your rabbit is dropping food, chewing with one side of the mouth, or avoiding certain foods, it could indicate dental issues. Likewise, excessive salivation can be a sign of mouth pain.

Respiratory Infections

Respiratory infections are caused by bacteria such as Pasteurella multocida. The symptoms are nasal discharge, sneezing, coughing, labored breathing, and conjunctivitis (inflammation of the eye lining). Stress, poor ventilation, and overcrowded living conditions can increase the likelihood of respiratory issues. During regular monitoring, observe your rabbit's breathing pattern. Rapid, labored, or noisy breathing can indicate a respiratory issue. In the case of a respiratory infection, you will also see clear or clouded discharge from the nose.

Pasteurellosis

Pasteurellosis is caused by the bacterium Pasteurella multocida. It often manifests as upper respiratory infections with symptoms like sneezing, nasal discharge, and eye discharge. However, it can also lead to more severe conditions such as abscesses (localized pus-filled swellings), particularly around the head and neck area. Rabbits with weakened immune systems are more susceptible to pasteurellosis. Always check for swelling around the head and neck region that can indicate the presence of abscesses.

Ear Mites

Ear mites are tiny parasites that infest a rabbit's ears, causing irritation, itching, and inflammation. Rabbits with ear mites may scratch their ears excessively, tilt their heads, and show signs of discomfort. Left untreated, ear mite infestations can lead to secondary bacterial infections and ear hematomas (blood-filled swelling in the ear flap). Regularly check the rabbits for ear scratching, redness, and swelling around the area covering the ears.

Myxomatosis

Myxomatosis is a viral disease that's usually spread by biting insects. It causes swelling and discharge around the eyes, ears, and genitalia. The virus weakens the rabbit's immune system, leaving them vulnerable to secondary bacterial infections. The disease progresses quickly and can be fatal within a week or two. Look for facial swelling where swollen eyes, ears, and face are characteristic signs. Furthermore, look out for watery or pus-like discharge from the eyes, nose, or genitalia.

Rabbit Hemorrhagic Disease (RHD)

RHD is a highly contagious viral disease that primarily affects the liver and blood vessels. It can lead to sudden death or internal bleeding, causing bloody discharge from the nose, mouth, or rectum. There are different strains of RHD, and its severity can vary. This disease poses a significant risk to unvaccinated rabbits. Watch for sudden death, as rabbits affected by RHD can die suddenly with no signs of disease. You should also look for bleeding from the nose, mouth, or rectum, and if you notice bloody discharge, immediately seek veterinary help.

E. cuniculi Infection

Encephalitozoon cuniculi is a microorganism that causes neurological issues in rabbits. It often affects the brain and kidneys. Infected rabbits will show symptoms such as a tilted head, seizures, incoordination, and urinary problems. The infection can be difficult to treat, leading to more chronic health problems. In case of an infection, there will be persistent head tilt or circling and difficulty walking.

Uterine Tumors

Female rabbits that haven't been spayed are at risk of developing uterine tumors, particularly adenocarcinomas. These tumors cause hormonal imbalances, uterine infections (pyometra), and pain. Spaying female rabbits at a young age will significantly reduce the risk of uterine problems. Swelling in the abdominal area and teeth grinding are some common signs that indicate uterine issues in female rabbits.

Skin Conditions

Rabbits can develop various skin issues, such as fur mites that cause itching and hair loss. Ringworm, a fungal infection, leads to circular areas of hair loss and skin inflammation. Abscesses are pus-filled swellings that occur anywhere on the body and are often caused by bacterial infections. Missing patches of hair and frequent scratching indicate the possibility of an underlying skin infection.

Obesity

Overfeeding and a diet high in carbohydrates leads to obesity. Obesity can result in joint problems, respiratory difficulties, and a reduced quality of life. It's essential to monitor a rabbit's diet and provide plenty of opportunities for exercise. Regularly assess your rabbit's body shape and weight. Overweight rabbits often have a round, bulging appearance.

Preventative Care Tips

Preventive care is essential to keep rabbits healthy and minimize the risk of common illnesses. Here are some vital tips for providing the best preventive care for your rabbit.

Proper Diet

Your rabbits should be provided with fresh, hygienic, and quality foods compatible with their tummies. Some recommendations include:

Hay

Rabbits should have access to high-quality grass at all times. Common hay types best for rabbits are timothy, meadow, and orchard grass. The essential fiber in the hay promotes health by helping rabbits digest food better.

Rabbits should have access to high-quality grass at all times.
https://www.pexels.com/photo/agriculture-arable-bale-countryside-289334/

Fresh Vegetables

Offer a variety of fresh, rabbit-safe veggies daily, like leafy greens (kale, romaine, parsley) and limited amounts of other veggies like carrots and bell peppers.

Limited Pellets

Although you can find several pellet varieties on the market, these pallets can never be used to substitute other foods. You can feed rabbits pallets that are high in fiber and low in calcium in limited quantities.

Water

Rabbits should always have access to fresh and clean water at all times. Not keeping the water clean increases the chances of transmittable diseases in the warren.

Regular Exercise

Allow your rabbits to have safe access to a larger space to exercise and explore, such as in a rabbit-proofed room or an exercise pen. You can provide toys like cardboard boxes, tunnels, and safe chew toys to keep your rabbits mentally and physically active.

Hygienic Housing Conditions

Clean your rabbit's living space regularly to prevent the buildup of waste and harmful microorganisms. A clean environment promotes good health and prevents the development and transmission of diseases. Surprisingly, your rabbits can also be litter trained, which makes cleanup easier. Depending on the breed, rabbits may need regular brushing to prevent matting and to remove loose fur. Densley-coated rabbit species with long fur will require daily grooming, whereas rabbits with short hair don't need much attention. Lastly, at least once a month, trim your rabbit's nails to prevent overgrowth and discomfort. Be careful never to cut below the quick.

Regular Vet Check-Ups

Find a veterinarian experienced with rabbits and schedule regular check-ups to catch any health issues early. Keep vaccinations up to date, including those for rabbit hemorrhagic disease (RHD) and myxomatosis.

Rabbit-Proofing

Make your home safe by securing cords, removing toxic plants, and blocking off access to dangerous areas.

Social Interaction

Rabbits are social animals. Spend time interacting with your rabbit daily to provide mental stimulation and companionship.

Weight Management

Monitor your rabbits' weight and body condition to prevent obesity. Adjust their diet and exercise routine accordingly.

Avoid Stress

Minimize stressors such as sudden changes in the environment, loud noises, or aggressive handling.

Parasite Prevention

Follow your vet's recommendations to prevent external parasites like fleas and mites.

Quarantine for New Additions

If you're introducing a new rabbit, quarantine them for a few weeks before introducing them to your existing rabbit(s) to prevent potential disease transmission.

Remember that rabbits have unique needs, and it's important to stay informed and educated about their care. Providing a well-rounded, balanced lifestyle with proper diet, exercise, hygiene, and medical attention will go a long way toward ensuring your rabbit's health and happiness.

Seeking Care

Knowing when to seek professional veterinary help is crucial for their well-being. If you notice any unusual behavior, symptoms, or changes in your rabbit's condition, it's best to consult a veterinarian experienced in rabbit care. Here are some guidelines on when to seek veterinary assistance and the types of treatments that might be necessary.

Emergency Situations

Seek immediate veterinary help if you observe any of the following:

- Severe difficulty breathing or gasping for air
- Sudden lethargy, weakness, or collapse
- Profuse bleeding from any part of the body
- Seizures or severe head tilt
- Distended belly, especially if accompanied by pain and discomfort
- Uncontrollable diarrhea or constipation
- Severe trauma or injury

Behavioral Changes

Rabbits are experts at hiding signs of illness. If you notice changes in behavior or routine, it could indicate a health problem:

- Decreased appetite or refusal to eat
- Reduced water intake
- Lethargy and reduced activity

- Isolation and hiding more than usual
- Teeth grinding (a sign of pain)
- Aggressive behavior or changes in social interaction

Gastrointestinal Issues

GI stasis, diarrhea, or constipation are common rabbit health issues.

- Seek help if your rabbit has not eaten or produced any fecal pellets for more than 12 hours.
- If your rabbit's stools are consistently soft or watery, or if they have difficulty passing stools.

Respiratory Symptoms

- Nasal discharge, sneezing, wheezing, labored breathing, and coughing can be signs of respiratory infections.
- If your rabbit is having trouble breathing or has a visible discharge, contact a vet.

Dental Problems

- If your rabbit is drooling, pawing at its mouth, or showing reluctance to eat, dental issues might be the cause.
- Overgrown teeth or dental spurs require professional trimming by a veterinarian.

Skin and Fur Issues

- Scratching, hair loss, scabs, or skin lesions could indicate mites, ringworms, or other skin conditions.
- Abscesses, lumps, or unusual growths should always be reported to a vet and examined.

Eye and Ear Issues

- Cloudy or bulging eyes, excessive tearing, redness, or discharge warrant veterinary attention.
- Head tilt, circling, and balance problems may indicate an inner ear infection or E. cuniculi infection.

Reproductive and Urogenital Issues

If you have an unspayed female rabbit, watch for signs of uterine issues like bleeding, swelling, or discomfort.

Male rabbits with difficulty urinating or producing urine could have urinary tract problems.

Vaccinations

Consult your vet about the recommended vaccination schedule for diseases like rabbit hemorrhagic disease (RHD) and myxomatosis. Treatments for rabbit health issues can vary widely and should always be determined by a veterinarian. They may include:

- Antibiotics or antiviral medications for infections
- Pain relief and anti-inflammatory medication
- Dental procedures for overgrown teeth or dental spurs
- Fluid therapy to combat dehydration
- Surgical procedures to remove abscesses or tumors
- Parasite treatment for external or internal parasites
- Supportive care such as syringe feeding, hydration, and temperature regulation

Vaccinations to Prevent Specific Diseases

The key is to seek professional veterinary care as soon as you notice any signs of illness or discomfort in your rabbit. Rabbits are delicate animals, and early intervention can make a significant difference in their prognosis and recovery.

Conduct in Emergency Situations

Stay Calm

In any emergency situation, staying calm is essential. Take a moment to collect yourself before taking action. Rabbits are sensitive to their owner's emotions, and your calm demeanor will help keep your rabbit from getting more stressed.

Assess the Situation

Quickly assess the situation to understand the severity of the emergency. Is your rabbit injured, showing signs of illness, or in immediate danger? This assessment will help you prioritize your actions.

Isolate and Protect

If your rabbit is in danger or is injured, gently move them to a safe and quiet area. Use a carrier or a confined space to prevent them from further harm or stress. Cover the carrier with a blanket to provide a sense of security.

Contact Your Veterinarian

Reach out to your veterinarian or an emergency veterinary clinic experienced with rabbits. Explain the situation and provide as much detail as possible about your rabbit's condition. Follow their advice and instructions closely.

First Aid

If your rabbit is bleeding or has an injury, use a clean, sterile cloth or gauze to apply gentle pressure to the affected area. Do not apply direct pressure to the eyes, nose, or mouth. Try to keep the area clean and minimize further trauma.

Breathing Difficulties

If your rabbit is having difficulty breathing, make sure they are in a well-ventilated area. Avoid drafts or extreme temperatures, as rabbits are sensitive to temperature changes. Keep them calm to reduce stress.

Stay Warm

In cases of shock or injury, your rabbit's body temperature can drop quickly. Cover them with a blanket or towel to help maintain their body heat. Be cautious not to overheat them, as rabbits can also become overheated.

Administer First Aid

Only administer first aid if you are trained – and it's safe. For example, if your rabbit is choking, clear their airways carefully. Always be gentle and avoid causing additional harm.

Transport to the Vet

If your veterinarian advises you to bring your rabbit in for immediate care, take them in as soon as possible. Secure a well-ventilated carrier in your vehicle to prevent sudden movements that could worsen their condition.

Keep Records

Document the symptoms you observed, the timeline of events, and any first aid you provided. These details will be valuable to the veterinarian in making an accurate diagnosis.

Follow Vet's Instructions

Follow your veterinarian's instructions carefully. They will guide you on how to stabilize your rabbit before you reach the clinic or tell you immediate steps to take.

Stay with Your Rabbit

If your rabbit requires hospitalization or treatment, stay in contact with the veterinary team. They will keep you informed about your rabbit's condition, treatment plan, and progress.

Remember, while you can provide some initial first aid, professional veterinary care is crucial for properly diagnosing and treating your rabbit's condition. Even if your rabbit seems to recover after first aid, it's still vital to seek professional assessment to ensure there are no hidden injuries or complications. Keeping your rabbit's safety and well-being a top priority in an emergency will help ensure the best possible outcome.

Owning a rabbit comes with the responsibility of safeguarding its health and well-being. These adorable creatures may be small, but they can be prone to health issues. By adopting a proactive approach to disease awareness and early management, you can ensure your rabbit enjoys a long and healthy life.

Understanding the Importance of Staying Informed

Being aware of common rabbit illnesses is essential. By understanding the signs and symptoms of conditions like gastrointestinal stasis, dental problems, and respiratory infections, you'll be better equipped to spot potential health concerns before they escalate.

Early Action

Recognizing warning signs is only the first step. Acting swiftly is crucial. If you notice any changes in your rabbit's behavior, appetite, or weight, don't hesitate to consult a veterinarian experienced in rabbit care. Your quick response can make all the difference in your rabbit's overall health.

Prioritizing Prevention

Preventing health issues is always preferable to treating them. Ensure your rabbit's diet is balanced and high in fiber, offer plenty of opportunities for exercise and mental stimulation, and keep its living space clean. Regular veterinary visits, vaccinations, and proactive grooming practices are also vital components of a preventive care routine.

Creating a Rabbit-Centric Lifestyle

Your rabbit's well-being should be at the center of your efforts. Make time to observe its behavior, engage in interactive play, and provide a comfortable and stress-free environment. By keeping your rabbit content and mentally stimulated, you contribute to its overall health.

Championing Your Rabbit's Health

As a responsible rabbit owner, you have the power to be your pet's health advocate. Taking a proactive approach to disease awareness and early management demonstrates your commitment to its happiness. Remember, your rabbit depends on you for its care. By prioritizing its health, you're ensuring that it enjoys a fulfilling life by your side.

Chapter 6: Ethical Breeding Practices for Sustainability

It can be tempting to just jump into raising rabbits and learn by going with the flow through trial and error. However, rabbits are living beings. Playing with the lives of the rabbits that will provide you with nourishment seems unnecessarily cruel. Therefore, ethical considerations must be taken into account when breeding rabbits. These considerations include health care, genetic diversity, housing, as well as understanding their reproductive cycles. By first gaining a deep understanding of the multiple factors that contribute to breeding healthy rabbits, you can make informed decisions to create the best environment for your rabbits. Sustainable backyard farming requires a conscious approach to animal rearing. Separating yourself from the often-cruel practices of large-scale industrial farming requires ethics to be applied to breeding and raising meat rabbits.

Rabbits are a lean source of protein, and they reproduce quickly. Setting up the frameworks to harness the fast rate of maturity in rabbits and the relatively cheap costs of raising them must align with a high ethical standard. Since you are raising your own meat, it is your responsibility to ensure that your animals live comfortably before slaughter. With a little bit of knowledge and by sticking to ethical principles, you can build a high-yield rabbit farm that takes up minimal space and is environmentally friendly. Once you have created your breeding system, it will be a lot easier to compassionately maintain a rabbit paradise. Therefore, exploring techniques to care for and breed rabbits ethically is central to an efficient backyard operation.

Managing Breeding Pairs

Understanding lineage is an essential component of ethical rabbit breeding. Ignoring genetic factors when breeding your animals could be disastrous and leave you with numerous defects and diseases. Choosing breeding pairs requires a basic comprehension of rabbit biology and their social behavior. Furthermore, there are many rabbit breeds to choose from, including the Flemish giant, the Californian, as well as the New Zealand White. Meat rabbits are chosen for their excellent bone-to-meat ratio, as well as their large size. It can be tempting to select the largest rabbits out of your litter for breeding to get more meat, but other factors determine which rabbits can be bred according to moral principles. A mindset driven by the quantity of meat production at the expense of quality could be a significant hindrance to crafting ethical backyard farming.

Understanding lineage is an essential component of ethical rabbit breeding.
https://www.pexels.com/photo/2-rabbits-eating-grass-at-daytime-33152/

Many breeders are profit-driven, which can often result in undesirable treatment of rabbits. If you are planning to sell rabbit meat or even breed them for your own consumption, one of the worst approaches you can take, ethically speaking, is to look at rabbits as a simple product. The aim is to give rabbits the most comfortable life before they are ultimately slaughtered for meat. The relationship between a breeder and their rabbits should be mutually beneficial. The breeding decisions you make will determine how well your rabbits socialize, how healthy they will be, and, eventually, how much yield you will get from them. Therefore, managing breeding requires in-depth attention to the genetic diversity of rabbits, preventing in-breeding, as well as sustaining a healthy population size that your housing and space can accommodate.

Genetic Diversity

The genetic diversity of your rabbits will largely depend on the type of breeding that you pursue. The main types of breeding for rabbits are line breeding, crossbreeding, outcrossing, and inbreeding. Crossbreeding is when you select rabbits from completely different breeds that have various characteristics and mix them so that you can maximize genetic diversity. The issue with crossbreeding is that you cannot register the rabbits with the American Rabbit Breeders Association because they are not purebred. Crossbreeding will limit the possible buyers for your rabbits because purebreds are more desirable on the market. Outcrossing addresses the problem of crossbreeding, producing lines that are not purebred. Out-crossing is breeding rabbits of the same breed from different lineages. Line-breeding refers to breeding rabbits from the same family. However, the breeder is careful to make decisions that create genetic diversity by mating rabbits that have some familial distance. For example, rabbits bred with line-breeding may be half-siblings, or grandchildren will be bred with grandparents. Inbreeding refers to members of the same litter breeding.

Outcrossing is one of the best methods to ethically breed rabbits. Crossbreeding creates genetic diversity. However, it could cause problems with birthing. For example, if a larger male breed mates with a smaller female breed, it can cause issues in the birthing process because the resulting mix could mean that the kits are too large for the mother. Line-breeding creates more consistency amongst your rabbits, and you have more control over choosing desirable characteristics, but it can lead to genetic inferiority if the technique is used long-term. Inbred rabbits are genetically similar, so litter can often be prone to disease or have some physical defects.

Preventing Inbreeding

Keeping track of where your breeding lines come from is one of the first steps toward preventing inbreeding. A simple way you can ensure your rabbits are not directly related is by buying rabbits from different farms. Bodies like the American Rabbit Breeders Association exist in part to keep track of the lineages and breeds of different rabbits. Therefore, to prevent inbreeding, you must be aware of where your rabbits are obtained. Furthermore, it is better to get rabbits from registered breeders because there is a paper trail that you can follow to see precisely where the lineages originate and how pure (or not) they are.

Once you have acquired your breeding rabbits, the most effective way to prevent inbreeding is to be observant. Depending on the breeds you are raising, the age of sexual maturity will be different. Once a rabbit has reached sexual maturity, they should be kept separate from their litter. It is also necessary to pay close attention to rabbit behavior. For example, a rabbit in heat will be more restless and exhibit behaviors such as rubbing its chin on its feed. Other physiological signs like a red, swollen vulva will also become apparent. Once your rabbits are sexually mature, they should be separated into breeding pairs and kept away from the litter they came from. Parents should not be allowed to mate with children, and brothers and sisters should also not be allowed to mate.

Sustaining a Healthy Population Size

Maintaining a healthy population size means that you should be aware of the maximum number of rabbits that can fit in the space that you have. You also need to be mindful of the doe-to-buck ratio and keep it balanced. For example, there should be about two bucks for about 20 does. When you are mating your bucks and doing so, you must be aware that the bucks can become territorial. Therefore, your does need to be moved into your buck's territory instead of moving your buck into a doe's territory where other bucks are present. A doe and her litter need at least six square feet of space to be healthy. Therefore, the surface area you have in which to raise your rabbits needs to be measured so you can calculate how many rabbits are your maximum capacity. Rabbits vary in size, so the space they need will change. An excellent way to measure if you have enough space for humane breeding is that each individual rabbit requires a section that is about five times bigger than its body.

Your breeding practices will also determine how healthy your population is. Genetic defects can leave you with a decreasing population. Therefore, when you mate any of your rabbits, you need to check if they are healthy and whether there is anything abnormal in their development. You want to use your strongest and healthiest bucks and does for mating. Furthermore, you should regularly change your bucks. Over time, your does will also begin producing smaller litters. Keeping track of your litter sizes is another way of making sure that a strong population is maintained.

Once your doe's litters begin to decrease significantly, it may be time to bring in younger does for breeding.

Reproductive Cycle

Ethical practices around the reproduction cycle are mainly concerned with the health of your breeding rabbits, as well as the conditions where breeding takes place. Rabbits are viable for breeding for about three years. It is suggested that you should swap your bucks at least once a year for optimal breeding. The span of a doe's pregnancy is about one month, depending on the breed. Once the kits are born, they nurse for approximately eight weeks. To ensure that your kits grow up healthily, they must breastfeed for the entire eight-week period. Kits can eat solid food at about two weeks old. However, this does not mean they are ready to stop drinking their mother's milk. A big part of ethical breeding is ensuring that you consider the health of your rabbits. Therefore, extensive care is needed for kits, as well as pregnant ones.

Once your doe has given birth and breastfed her kits, you need to make sure that she is healthy before breeding her again. Pregnancy takes a lot out of a doe. You can check her energy levels, as well as her body, for any injuries before breeding her again. You need to wait at least 35 days before rebreeding your doe after the litter has been weaned. This will protect the health of your doe, as well as the health of any future litter. Sometimes, a pseudo-pregnancy can occur, which lasts for about 17 days. This can happen if a doe mates with a sterile male or from other physical stimulation. Therefore, it's essential to monitor a pregnant doe if you want to maintain a healthy population.

Appropriate Breeding Ages

Rabbits are ready to breed from anywhere between four to seven months, depending on their size and their breed. Smaller breeds tend to mature faster. For almost all breeds, bucks mature much slower than they do. When your rabbits are ready for breeding, it is crucial to track their mating patterns to ensure that both the does and bucks remain healthy. A buck should be allowed to mate at least every three to four days. Healthy bucks can continue mating for about two to three years, but for a strong lineage, it is suggested that your mating bucks get swapped at least once a year. Unlike many other mammal species, rabbits do not ovulate according to a set schedule. Does only ovulate when there is sexual stimulation.

Commercial rabbit farms produce about five to six liters a year. For ethical breeding practices, your breeding should not be strictly driven by maximizing litters. Your dose should be monitored to make sure that they are healthy and strong enough to produce more litters. You do not want to put too much strain on your animals if your aim is to increase their quality of life. Although your rabbits are essentially a commodity, for your breeding practices to hold a high ethical standard, you must consider the rabbits' quality of life. Therefore, your rabbits should only be bred when they are in optimal health, and you should prevent overbreeding.

Caring for Pregnant Does

Pregnancy is a vulnerable time for most mammals. So, a higher degree of care is needed when a doe is pregnant. There are various ways to tell when a doe is pregnant. One of the more obvious ways to detect it is by checking the size of the abdomen. The body weight will also significantly increase. Another way of checking is by placing a buck near her. Bucks will not mate with those who are already pregnant. When a rabbit gives birth, it is known as kindling. Before kindling occurs, it is important to build a nest.

Sometimes, it can be difficult for a doe to conceive. This indicates that either the buck or the doe is unhealthy, and one of the main causes of a doe being unable to conceive is if she is overweight. Since it is ethical to maintain optimal health for your rabbits, you must ensure that your rabbits are at a healthy size. Overweight bucks also tend to lose libido and are lazy. Old age, disease, and injuries can prevent rabbits from breeding effectively. So, it makes sense that you keep your rabbits in tip-top condition.

Caring for Newborn Kits

Rabbits care for their young very well. Your duty as a breeder is to make sure that the conditions for caring are set up appropriately. Rabbits use their fur to make nests for their kits. You can add sawdust to the enclosure for the doe to use to construct a nest as well. Sometimes, rabbits can get orphaned. Maybe the doe got injured or died during the kindling process. If this happens, you will have to bottle-feed the baby rabbits using a special formula. A great substitute for rabbit milk is kitten milk. You will also need to construct the nest yourself.

Researching what is best for your rabbits is not a once-off activity. As you continue on your breeding journey, you will need to do continuous research. Keeping yourself up to date with the latest information is the cornerstone of ethical breeding practices. There are always new information and best practice updates available. For the most part, caring for newborn kits simply means checking on them daily and making sure that the mother is healthy because they are natural nurturers. If you notice any concerning changes or behavior that is outside of the norm, conducting research is beneficial. Through keen observation and staying updated with scientific developments, you can maintain a healthy herd.

Health Considerations

You choose the rabbits you raise; they don't choose you. Therefore, any health concerns land firmly on your shoulders. Rabbit meat is cheap, and rabbits are relatively easy to raise. However, that does not mean that they are able to remain resilient when their health is neglected. Rabbit health is primarily based on three factors: housing, nutrition, and maintenance. By grooming your animals, feeding them well, and creating a shelter that caters to their basic needs, you can ethically raise rabbits that will provide you with ample meat for profit or consumption. There are differences between raising rabbits for pets and raising rabbits for meat. Meat rabbits are bigger than rabbits bred for pets. Furthermore, there are differences in the care they need.

Meat rabbits will inevitably be slaughtered. However, just because they will be killed for their meat doesn't mean their lives must be filled with suffering. The better rabbits are taken care of, the healthier they will be. Healthy rabbits produce higher-quality meat that will taste better and can be sold at a premium. So, keeping your rabbits healthy is beneficial all around because they will have a higher quality of life, and it is beneficial to you because you will have a higher-quality end product. Ethical health considerations may take more time and effort, but it is worth it for the animal welfare, as well as the premium meat that you will enjoy.

Nutrition

Commercially available rabbit feed in the form of pellets has all the necessary nutrients to maintain a healthy diet. Using commercial rabbit feed is more advisable than trying to mix your own feed because it has been scientifically formulated. Treating your rabbits with some leafy greens or veggies occasionally is okay, but commercial pellets are sufficient for all their dietary needs. Additionally, water must always be readily available for the rabbit. Since rabbits are susceptible to extreme temperatures, a lot more water is needed in the summer to help them cool down and control their body temperature.

Commercially available rabbit feed in the form of pellets has all the necessary nutrients to maintain a healthy diet.

Housing

Rabbits are sensitive to extreme temperature changes. Therefore, housing is one of the main factors that contribute to healthy rabbits. Increases in cold or heat can cause rabbits to die or become infertile. Enclosures must also be built in a way that blocks the wind. The combination of wind and cold is devastating for rabbits, and you could end up losing your entire herd. Ethically, as a breeder, you must create a comfortable space for your rabbits. A well-kept rabbit enclosure allows your rabbits to be comfortable, safe, and free from injuries and diseases.

In addition to maintaining warmth for your rabbits, fencing is a central part of rabbit housing. Many people make the mistake of thinking that fencing is primarily meant to keep rabbits in, so they buy the cheapest fencing from their local garden store. This approach is completely wrong. Any fencing that is installed must be predator-proof. Rabbits are vulnerable to all kinds of predators, including foxes, coyotes, dogs, cats, and various birds of prey. Your fencing should be geared around keeping predators out more than keeping your rabbits in. It is not ethical to put your rabbits in harm's way because it's your job to ensure their safety. Healthy and safe living conditions for your rabbits are the crucial pillars for breeding rabbits ethically.

Medical Care

Preventing illness, disease, and injury is centered upon creating sanitary conditions for your rabbits. Your rabbits and the environment that they live in must be kept clean at all times. Rabbits have sensitive ears and nails, which means that you need to check on them regularly. Furthermore, you need to keep your rabbit's nails short. When clipping their rabbit, make sure you don't nick any arteries by cutting below the quick. This is excruciatingly painful for the rabbit, and it could become infected. Getting regular checkups from a vet is also advisable. If one of your rabbits gets a disease or illness, they can likely spread it to all your rabbits. So regular vet checkups are advisable so that you can pick up on any illnesses early on.

Chapter 7: The Life Cycle of a Rabbit

Understanding the life cycle of rabbits is essential to maintain a high-functioning breeding operation. At different times of their lives, rabbits display certain behaviors and needs. To provide their rabbits with the best care to produce quality meat, a breeder needs to be acutely aware of the stages of rabbit life. There are four main stages of developmental evolution: the kit or newborn, the juvenile, the adult, and the senior phase. Grasping the intricacies of each phase of the rabbit life cycle helps a breeder make informed decisions that will benefit their herd and, ultimately, their meat.

At each stage of their life cycle, rabbits will have specific needs. A breeder must effectively meet these needs, and breeding healthy rabbits requires an in-depth understanding of their biological functioning. Age plays a big role in the biology of a rabbit. Considering that a breeder interacts with rabbits from birth to adulthood, understanding what rabbit behavior and functioning is normal at each age can help them determine how fit their herd is. A healthy herd leads to better meat or more profit if a breeder aims to sell their rabbits.

Kit

The kit stage is when a rabbit is at its most vulnerable.

The kit stage is when a rabbit is at its most vulnerable. Kits require specialized care from both the breeder and its mother. Knowing exactly what a healthy kit looks like and how it behaves leads to more informed breeding decisions and interventions that might be needed at this early stage of life. When you are breeding rabbits, there will be a constant cycle of newborns that need your attention. The nutritional requirements of the kits, coupled with housing and medical care, create a matrix of focused attention needed to assure the best possible outcomes for your herd.

The kit or newborn stage is from birth to about three months old. Typically, at this part of the rabbit life cycle, a high level of care is needed from the dam or the mother rabbit. The fragile babies clumsily scurry around, clueless about the dangers of the pen. The sire, or the father rabbit, does not play a pivotal role at this level of development. Kits are born with their eyes closed and have no fur at the early stages. Their body heat cannot be maintained, so they are kept warm by the dam and a nest. Breeders need to provide sawdust, which the dam will use together with her fur to keep her young warm.

For the first two weeks, kits acquire nutrition that comes predominantly from milk. After the first two weeks, they will start eating pellets. However, they are not ready to be weaned off milk until about eight weeks. A newborn rabbit will be two to three inches long and will weigh 30 to 40 grams. These gorgeous babies feed once or twice a day for five to ten minutes per feeding. The nutrient-rich milk provides the appropriate sustenance for a young rabbit on one feeding every 24 hours. Kits will usually feed early in the morning, between midnight and 5 a.m.

Since newborn kits are so vulnerable, it is essential to check on them consistently, especially immediately after the birth. The dam sometimes leaves the nest unattended, which is a perfect time to check on the little ones. Unfortunately, it is common for the babies to die early on, so this is an opportunity to remove any dead kits. Handling the nest must be done with extreme caution so as not to disturb them too much. A dam will eat the placenta after birth, but sometimes, the cleanup can be a bit sloppy. Assist mom by removing any leftover placenta when you are checking on the newborn kits. Once you have made sure that all the kits are healthy and alive, you can check if they have been fed. A dam can have a problem feeding kits, so they will have to be bottle-fed. If they have been fed, their bellies will be round and protruding. If you disturb the nest, it is essential to restore it to the way you found it.

The young ones will finally be ready to leave the nest at about two to three weeks old. At this point, they begin eating pellets and will not be exclusively reliant on their mother's milk. After six to eight weeks, your kits can be removed from their mother and weaned off milk. The babies will now be much more independent and will not require the focused care they once did. However, rabbits are still considered kits up until about three months old. Although these young ones are not as vulnerable as they once were, it is still necessary to check on them regularly to monitor their health.

For the health of the dam, weaning should be done gradually. When kits are abruptly removed, this can cause the development of mastitis. Mastitis is a disease that results in the swelling of the breast of the rabbit. This swelling can lead to infection, resulting in the mother's premature death. Although the sire or the father is not as integral to the development of the kits as the mother is, it can also help to keep the sire around for the first few weeks to prevent stressing out the babies or the dam. The father acts as a stable foundational support for your breeding family.

Juvenile

Once a kit has grown significantly, it transitions into a juvenile. This stage can be likened to a human teenager. The juvenile phase is the bridging period between being a kit and reaching adulthood. This stage starts from about three months old up until about a year. Some of the bigger breeds reach adulthood earlier, at about nine months old. Feed becomes more important as hungry teenagers consistently munch to support their rapid growth. Alfalfa hay and quality pellets are a good feed to use at this stage of development because it is so calcium-rich and will help adolescents develop strong bones and muscles. It's also high in fiber, which aids in digestion.

At this stage, feeding should be constant, with a consistent flow of pellets readily available. The explosive growth of juvenile rabbits requires nutrients, so they feed often. The most important consideration for raising rabbits at this age is making sure that they have ample food and water readily available. A good balance must be maintained by providing free-flowing feed and, at the same time, preventing overeating because these young ones can be gluttonous. The chubby juveniles can sometimes be prone to gorging themselves. You need to develop a feeding protocol that makes sure that the rabbits are well-fed while not allowing them to overindulge.

Juvenile rabbits are very active, so they require a lot of space to run around. Creating an enclosure with different levels that the rabbits can hop around on will help manage their high energy levels. As they transition to adulthood, they experience hormonal changes, and you'll notice they become much more aggressive. Young rabbits may exhibit unruly behavior like damaging their enclosure, biting, or spraying urine everywhere. Therefore, these unpredictable guys must be monitored to make sure that they do not hurt themselves or other rabbits. Biting can cause injury or infection, so check to make sure that your rabbits do not have wounds caused by your hormonal juveniles.

Rabbits that are kept for pets are often neutered when they reach this juvenile phase because of their hyperactive behavior, like biting, digging, and moving around frantically. This behavior must be tolerated by a breeder because you need these misbehaved rabbits to reproduce. So, any shelter that is built for these teenage nightmares should take into account the rebellious and active nature of rabbits at this age. You can also expect more fights from adolescent rabbits due to their hormonal changes. At this developmental phase, the mischievous rabbits tend to express aggressive territorial behavior. They will lunge at you when you enter their space, so you have to be careful when handling them.

The curiosity, aggression, and hyperactivity that grow in the juvenile phase of rabbit development will subside with age. These behaviors are influenced by the raging hormones of puberty. Juvenile rabbits are moving closer to sexual maturity. In male rabbits, you may find that they begin mounting objects or other rabbits. This is a normal sign of development for a young rabbit. After the age of one, they will step into adulthood, so they will calm down significantly from the peak of the rambunctious transitionary stage of their life cycle. Male rabbits are more aggressive than females and are the ones who express the most territorial and aggressive behaviors.

Hormonal shifts also play a role in female rabbits. As juveniles, female rabbits may begin nesting. Adult rabbits only nest when they are ready to give birth. When young females begin nesting, it is a sign of false pregnancy. The rabbit is getting ready to start mating. Rabbits do not ovulate when there are no males around. The hormonal changes are preparing the animal for sexual maturity and the biological demands that come with it.

The primary concerns when rabbits are at the juvenile phase are preventing fighting and maintaining their living spaces. Juvenile rabbits are prone to damaging property by chewing and digging. Furthermore, your animals may need vaccinations at this early stage to prevent the spread of various diseases. It is advised to either have a vet do a home visit or to take your herd to the vet so that a medical professional can make sure that they have no injuries or life-threatening diseases. If a small number of rabbits get sick in your herd, they can likely spread the illnesses. Therefore, getting all the necessary vaccinations early on is highly recommended.

Adult

When rabbits reach adulthood, it means that they will no longer increase in size.
https://www.pexels.com/photo/white-rabbit-wearing-yellow-eyeglasses-4588065/

Depending on the breed of the rabbit, adulthood is reached between the ages of nine months to 18 months. This is when your rabbits are fully grown and ready to begin breeding. The life span of a rabbit is from about three to nine years; therefore, most of a rabbit's life will be spent as an adult. Meat rabbits called fryers are usually slaughtered before they reach adulthood at the ages of about three to six months old. The adult rabbits that you have will predominately be used as breeders. Some people deem it more ethical to wait for a rabbit to reach adulthood before they get slaughtered or sold for meat.

When rabbits reach adulthood, it means that they will no longer increase in size. Now that you know your rabbits will not get any bigger, you can calculate the dimensions of your enclosures according to the mass of the mature rabbits. In adulthood, rabbits are not as aggressive as they were when they were juveniles, but they can still display some of the same behaviors, like being territorial. Considering that your adult rabbits are your breeding rabbits, they are essentially the center of your operation. Therefore, specialized care is needed to make sure that they are able to breed well.

Food for adult rabbits needs to be strictly controlled. Unlike juvenile rabbits that are still growing, adult rabbits have reached their full size, so their food supply will be steadier. High-quality pellets and hay are all that is needed to feed adult rabbits. In addition to the food, they should also have readily available water. Rabbits tend to become lazier when they get older, so there is a risk of obesity, which can affect their fertility. Since your adults are your breeders, it is essential to make sure that they maintain a healthy, productive weight to maximize litter sizes.

The rabbits maturing to adulthood are carefully selected by breeders. Your adult rabbits should have all the most desirable traits that you intend to pass on to future generations. All the rabbits that you keep until adulthood should be the strongest, fittest, and healthiest out of your litter. These are the rabbits that are not prone to injury or illness and can produce the most meat. Therefore, you must be carefully selective of the rabbits that you sell or consume and the ones that you keep for breeding. Usually, there are about two bucks to twenty does, so you will have to select your rabbits according to gender as well.

Considering that adult rabbits can become lazy, which could lead to them gaining weight, your enclosure needs to be structured in a way that encourages activity. Installing some moving parts into your housing can be beneficial because a repetitive environment can cause boredom amongst adult rabbits, which will fuel their lazy proclivities. When you have sections that can move around and allow you to rearrange your enclosures, it will prevent laziness and keep your rabbits active. Movable parts that you can install in your enclosures can be simple, like steps, boxes, or tunnels for your rabbits to play in. Nutrition and exercise are the two most important factors when caring for adult rabbits.

Sick rabbits, or animals with genetic deficiencies, will usually be culled before they reach adulthood. Some rabbits with deformities can still be sold for meat. Considering that your genetic selection will make sure that you have a powerful bloodline of adult-breeding rabbits, it will not be difficult to care for them at this age. Besides cleaning, feeding, and checking for injuries, adult rabbits are relatively low maintenance when compared to newborns, juveniles, and even senior rabbits.

In adulthood, your rabbits will become a lot less active after about three years. This is when aging starts to kick in, and they are transitioning to the senior geriatric phase. This is why it is suggested that your breeding males should be swapped at least once every year. Furthermore, as females age, their litters will also become smaller. Therefore, when your rabbits are adults, you need to monitor how active they are, as well as the size of the litter, so that you can make profitable breeding decisions. Adult rabbits are low maintenance, but the care you give them will determine how long they can effectively breed.

Senior

For a breeder, it is unlikely that their rabbits will reach the senior phase of life. Rabbits are considered geriatric between the ages of five and seven. At this age, your rabbits are close to natural death. Therefore, as a breeder, your animals will get sold off before they reach this late stage of life. However, if you keep some rabbits until they are geriatric, they do have specific needs that are unique to elders. Thus, you will need to adjust your care once any of your rabbits have reached this stage of their life. The needs of senior rabbits are excessive, and it could be compared to the level of care needed at the newborn level.

A senior rabbit is going to be a pet. No profitable benefits are attached to caring for a senior. When a rabbit becomes geriatric, they are no longer able to breed. They can be sold for slaughter, but meat rabbits are sold long before they reach this stage. Old rabbits become even less active than adult rabbits as their health begins to slowly deteriorate. Many people keep older rabbits for pets because of how calm they are. Senior rabbits are highly unlikely to lunge at you like juveniles and do not exhibit the same kinds of territorial behavior. Moreover, they are not damaging to enclosures because they are so inactive. Senior rabbits eat less than adult rabbits because their appetites decrease with age.

Geriatric rabbits are difficult to take care of because they experience a number of diseases and ailments. These elders can have ear issues, renal failure, arthritis, eye problems, and dental diseases. Female rabbits that have been breeders and have not been spayed can also develop uterine tumors. Therefore, visits from the vet will be common for senior rabbits. Older rabbits are fragile and require constant care. Since they no longer breed, keeping a senior rabbit is a liability to a breeding operation, so if you are going to keep rabbits until they get this old, you need to be aware that they will cost you money.

Older rabbits tend to get scared easily, so you'll need to keep them in a stress-free environment. Geriatric rabbits can suffer from heart failure when they are frightened or startled. Rabbits are social creatures, but keeping a senior rabbit around many adults and juvenile rabbits could be fatal because of how high the stimuli in that kind of environment are. Any decisions you make about the living conditions of your senior rabbits will have to include considerations for the fragile heart conditions of the vulnerable older rabbits.

To extend the life of a senior rabbit, the environment it lives in must be comfortable. Senior rabbits also need some exercise, but, for the most part, they will be lazy. A soft environment with carpets and cushioning is ideal to prevent injury, as well as provide some comfort in movement because their joints may be sensitive. The loss of mobility caused by their deteriorating joints means that they will not be able to groom themselves well. Therefore, if you are keeping older rabbits, you will need to groom them and give them dry baths.

Senior rabbits rapidly lose weight as they begin losing their appetite. It becomes essential to feed senior rabbits with high-quality and nutrient-dense food. The loss of appetite that older rabbits experience contributes to them rapidly losing weight. Caring for senior rabbits means that you consistently have to check their physical condition because changes can happen quickly. While you are grooming a senior rabbit, you can check for any lumps or injuries because these can be indicators of a number of diseases. Furthermore, senior rabbits need their nails trimmed more often because their inactivity allows for their nails to grow a lot longer. The combination of grooming, nutrition, medical care, and checking for injuries is the reason senior rabbits require more attention than younger rabbits.

Chapter 8: Compassionate Harvesting

Breeding rabbits for meat means that, at some point, your animals will be harvested. Furthermore, some of your herd will need to be euthanized for various other reasons like population control, genetic defects, or diseases. Killing does not need to be cruel. Breeding rabbits for meat makes killing unavoidable, but there are ways to ethically approach the process of harvesting. Educating yourself on the most humane practices in the industry can help you set up a more compassionate operation. Your animals provide you with meat or income at the expense of their lives. Therefore, you are responsible for making sure that your rabbits have the best experience possible before they are forced to make the ultimate sacrifice.

Any unnecessary distress needs to be eradicated from your breeding operations. This suffering includes injuries and prolonged deaths. Slaughtering and euthanasia should be done in the most painless ways possible. The ASPCA says that for a slaughter to be considered humane, the death has to be painless, or the animal's senses must be numbed (Browning and Veit, 2020). Furthermore, the ASPCA also advocates for instantaneous death that is free from agony (Browning and Veit, 2020). Numerous measures can be taken to ensure that your breeding setup meets or exceeds these standards.

In addition to painless slaughter and euthanasia, the conditions in which they live leading up to the killing of your animals must also be taken into account. Your rabbits need to be kept calm and must be put at ease before slaughter. Therefore, using humane handling techniques and crafting a slaughtering environment that is geared toward compassionate killing is crucial to running an ethical backyard farm. Many people are driven to backyard farming to produce their own meat because of some of the atrocious practices that are widespread throughout factory farming. Farming meat rabbits sustainably and conscientiously requires you to embrace reform in the farming industry by implementing change on a small scale.

Educating yourself on the most humane practices in the industry can help you set up a more compassionate operation.

Compassionate harvesting does not begin at the butchering table but encompasses all your breeding practices. The reduction of stress before butchering is incumbent on the conditions that your animals live under. Therefore, a safe, sanitary, and spacious environment is the initial step to compassionate harvesting. Compassion implies a high level of care for your rabbits. Thus, the killing process must be conducted with the utmost respect for the animals. There is no truly kind way to kill an animal. However, you can get as close as possible to humane by being principle-driven over commodity-driven. Rabbits are mammals, so people can somewhat relate to their ability to experience pain and suffer as sentient creatures. The connection you have with your rabbits as living beings providing you with sustenance in the form of meat or profit must be shown through caring practices.

Inhumane slaughter and euthanasia, where animals experience excessive pain and suffering, can be reduced by effective training and information. Human error is largely to blame for inducing animal suffering through cruel slaughter practices and mistakes being made in the stunning process. Getting professional assistance and working toward being competent in slaughtering and euthanasia can prevent animal anguish. The rabbit industry is largely unregulated due to the meat not being as popular as beef, chicken, or mutton. However, this weak regulation should not encourage cruel practices. The lack of proper regulation in the rabbit breeding industry should be an encouragement to hold yourself to an even higher standard as you are in the position to contribute to industry standards as a way-paver.

Humane Methods of Euthanasia

Rabbits have complex physical, social, and psychological needs. When killing rabbits, you should consider all these multiple variables if you aim to make the breeding operation ethical and humane. Slaughtering animals for meat may seem like the primary concern of killing animals. However, breeding will sometimes require killing for other reasons. Profitability is a goal for many breeding operations. There are times when it can be difficult to sell rabbits, which could result in the need for some animals to be culled.

Overpopulation in a small space is a form of animal cruelty. Therefore, euthanizing rabbits can be perceived as a way to show mercy to your herd. The process of selectively reducing your population is called culling. There are two types of culling when it comes to meat rabbit breeding, namely hard culling and soft culling. Soft culling is when your rabbit population is not killed. A soft cull includes selling rabbits for pets or halting breeding activities. Hard culling refers to euthanizing your rabbits. When you cull your animals, you will choose weaker rabbits that have defects or seem to be more prone to sickness.

There are a variety of ways that breeders select which rabbits will be culled. One of them is the elimination of those without mothering instincts. Sometimes, a dam will abandon its motherly duties like cleaning its kits after birth. Dams without mothering instincts often trample or eat their young. Many breeders go by the three-strike rule, meaning that if a rabbit displays an inability to mother three times, it puts the animal in a position for culling. People get attached to the animals they raise, so this can be a difficult decision to make. A meat rabbit breeding operation is dissimilar from a sanctuary or pet breeding operation in the sense that culling can become part of the business model.

The most common way to euthanize a rabbit is by putting it under anesthesia, whether this is through inhalation or by injection, and then proceeding to decapitate the rabbit. The rabbit will not experience any pain or suffering when this method is used. Another way that rabbits are euthanized is by lethal injection into their main vein. This method also painlessly kills the rabbit. These methods of euthanasia are conducted by a qualified vet. It can be dangerous to attempt these methods yourself as an unqualified person because a mistake can result in the prolonged suffering of a rabbit.

Using a vet to euthanize your rabbits can be expensive, so some breeders will opt to euthanize their own animals. For young kits, it is easier to kill them because they are smaller and more fragile. A swift motion with a sharp knife to decapitate a rabbit, starting from the spine downwards, can end the animal's life relatively painlessly. With older rabbits, using a knife is not as humane because the spine is strong enough to prevent a clean cut. With younger rabbits, you can also use the bowl method for euthanasia. The bowl method is sometimes used by pet shops for culling mice and rabbits, which are fed to snakes. Place the bowl on the back of a kit's neck. Push down hard on the bowl while you pull the kit's hind legs. This method dislocates the kit's cervical, which produces an instant kill. Some people use carbon dioxide chambers to euthanize rabbits, but this method is undesirable because death is slow.

Compassionate Butchering

Your rabbits are bred for meat, so they will need to be slaughtered at some point. You can outsource the slaughter to a more skilled individual, or you can learn how to slaughter the rabbits yourself. When you outsource your butchering, there are two main factors to consider. Firstly, the person that you appoint must be knowledgeable about how to kill your animals without causing suffering. Secondly, some cost considerations need to be made because you will most likely be paying for the service.

Therefore, if you are selling your rabbit meat, the slaughtering process will need to be accounted for in your sales price.

You have the option of selling your live rabbits to butchers. If you take this option, you need to also do some research about the condition of the slaughterhouse. It is advisable to do a tour of the place to see if it meets your ethical standards. The rabbits will need to be stunned before killing, or if they are not numbed, a sharp knife should be used to ensure that the kill is instant. Moreover, it is essential to check the cleanliness of the abattoir because unsanitary conditions can cause further suffering of animals and contamination of the meat, which causes discomfort for the people who consume the product.

Homestead breeders also use a variety of other methods for slaughtering rabbits. One of the more prominent methods is using a blunt object to hit the rabbit hard on the head. Hitting the rabbit on the head causes the animal to be knocked unconscious. After the rabbit is knocked out, a sharp knife will be used to cut one of the main arteries in its throat and bleed it out. The problem with using blunt force to knock a rabbit out is that if you hit the rabbit incorrectly and the strike is not precise, the rabbit will not be knocked unconscious with the first hit. Suppose the rabbit is not made unconscious after the first blow. In that case, multiple blows will be needed to knock the animal out, which causes pain and trauma before slaughtering.

The most humane method of slaughtering is dislocating the cervical (neck). To do this, use a sharp knife to cut the spine while the rabbit's hind legs are pulled. This method is more difficult to use on older rabbits because their spines are stronger, so the knife has to be extremely sharp, and a lot of pressure must be applied. Furthermore, the method takes skill, so it is unlikely that a beginner will be able to painlessly slaughter a rabbit using this method. If you are going to dislocate the cervical of your animals to ensure an instant kill, it's best to do it with the guidance of a professional familiar with the process. A few lessons before attempting the method on your own could be highly beneficial to maintain a great ethical standard.

Rabbits are social animals, so removing those you are slaughtering away from the group is recommended to reduce stress. Furthermore, considering that rabbits can be prone to heart problems, as well as being sensitive to extreme temperatures, it is essential to make sure that the environment for slaughter is calm and temperature controlled. Your rabbit should be restrained properly to prevent movement, which could lead to inaccurate slicing that harms the animal. The conditions that you slaughter the animal under are just as important as your slaughtering technique.

Minimizing Stress

The stress of rabbits is often related to the environment in which they are raised. Many breeding operations use small cages crammed into limited space so that profit can be maximized. This creates a stressful environment for rabbits where they can exhibit antisocial behaviors like hurting themselves and others. Rabbits are socially and psychologically complex and need to be placed in a humane environment to allow them to thrive. One of the more humane ways of raising rabbits is called cuniculture farming. In this form of rabbit breeding, the animals are given space to graze naturally as if they were in the wild. This can be more costly because more space is required for fewer rabbits to be produced. However, this is one of the best ways to give a rabbit a stress-free life before it gets slaughtered.

The enclosure that your rabbits are kept in should be clean, spacious, and safe. Having an unsafe environment could result in your rabbits picking up illnesses or getting injured. These diseases and injuries that occur in inhumane living environments add to the suffering that rabbits experience before getting slaughtered. An acceptable enclosure should have enough space for rabbits to move around in and should preferably have multiple levels for rabbits to jump on and crawl through. The fencing should also be installed in a way that has no protruding parts that can cut or injure the rabbits. Humane slaughtering conditions require sufficient housing.

Since rabbits are social, interacting with them often can build enough trust that your presence calms them down. Grooming your rabbits and interacting with them during feeding can help them to bond with you. The connection you establish by building a relationship with your rabbits means they will be calmer when they are taken to get slaughtered. As a compassionate breeder, you must reduce rabbit suffering all the way until they end up on the chopping block.

The psychological state is just as important as the physical condition. Rabbits that are in a poor mental condition could be further impacted physically. The behavior of your rabbits will show you the mental condition that they are in. For example, distressed animals will have altered toilet habits and will chew on their cage or even repeatedly circle their enclosure. When herd members exhibit these kinds of behaviors, it may be a sign to adjust the way that you are caring for the animals. Maximizing the comfort of your rabbits will impact your final product by giving you high-quality meat because the mental and physical health of the rabbits contribute to how they develop.

If the environment that you are breeding your rabbits in is stress-free for the animals, it can also support your breeding operation by providing bigger litter. Fertility can be linked to psychology because distressed rabbits can have heart issues that impact their mating. It is not only the rabbits that benefit from consideration for their mental state, but you as well because your breeding rabbits will produce bigger and healthier litters if their mental state is at ease. By keeping a calm and healthy environment, you can produce meat to be sold at a premium. Having premium meat available can be profitable, especially considering that the rabbit meat market is smaller than other domestic animals like chickens, sheep, or cows.

Ethical Animal Treatment

The need to butcher and euthanize animals painlessly to prevent suffering is built upon the principle of ethical animal treatment. Many organizations in the farming industry create regulations that govern how farmers can treat animals. Various activist groups challenge some of these regulations because they are conscious of the well-being of animals. Since the rabbit breeding industry is not as strictly governed as other meat farms, the ethical treatment of your animals is placed on the shoulders of individual breeders. The initiative to take the precautions to build a humane backyard farm is largely driven by your own ethical approach.

Research into the psychology and complex societal structures of rabbits can be used as a guiding tool to create an ethical farm where compassionate harvesting is promoted. The aim is to understand rabbits enough to create an environment where they are able to physically and psychologically flourish. Although your rabbits are, in essence, a commodity, that does not mean that their well-being should be ignored. It is in your best interest to treat your rabbits ethically because healthier rabbits will produce better meat.

Breeders have an obligation to be caring – and various regulatory bodies govern how you can treat your animals. Aligning with the law is only the first step in being ethical. Compassionate harvesting implies that there is an emotional connection to the animals that you breed. Bigger scale operations tend to create a coldness due to the methodological factory approach they have to breeding and slaughtering rabbits. As a backyard breeder, you are in the unique position of using the small-scale nature of your breeding operation to create a more personalized style of care. Unlike your factory farm counterparts, you can take the time to care for each individual rabbit to make sure that they are living their best lives.

The emotional connection you establish with your animals, coupled with being well-researched, informed, and educated, builds the foundation for compassionate harvesting. The difference between compassion and indifference is the ability to feel the pain of others. Therefore, establishing a strong bond backed by scientifically informed knowledge can put you in a position to understand the pain and desires of your rabbits. From the ledge of understanding, you can overlook a backyard breeding setup that is humane, profitable, and functional.

Chapter 9: Using Rabbit By-Products

Rabbit meat, when compared to other meat, is a rich source of protein and is healthier than most. Beyond their delicious meat, rabbits are also cultivated for their by-products – which are profitable and can give you a regular income stream. Therefore, this chapter teaches the ethical and efficient use of all parts of the rabbit and the beneficial use of rabbit manure for gardening. Additionally, you will be guided on using other by-products like bone and organs.

Ethical and Efficient Use of All Parts of the Rabbit

Head: In some countries, the head and brain of rabbits are eaten. Recipes like spicy Sichuan Rabbit Head and Rabbit Head Paste are examples of recipes using the head and brain. Traditionally, rabbit head is used in stews and for stock. They are also used to feed dogs, pigs, and chickens. Rabbit heads are crushed for chicken feeds with the blood, meat, and bone regarded as a good choice for feeding laying hens.

The rabbit brain is used in the pelt tanning process. It is believed that the brain size of every animal is sufficient to tan the pelt of that animal. Furthermore, the brain is a rich source of omega-3 fatty acids.

Ear: Rabbits ears are dehydrated and used as a dog treats. They can also be deep-fried and eaten with apricot ginger chutney sauce.

Pelts: It produces blankets, headgear, coats, hats, and other clothing for keeping warm. They can be added to clothing as trimming.

Feet: You can turn rabbit feet into a lucky charm by drying them and adding some cool decorative items. You can do this by adding in a small jar 70% isopropyl rubbing alcohol. Soak the feet completely in the alcohol solution for two days, creating a lock in the fur. This alcohol will dehydrate the cells, killing fungus and bacteria. Rinse with clean water after two days. Mix some borax with water to a ratio of 15 to 1. You can use hot water to get the borax to dissolve quickly. With its antibacterial and antifungal properties, the borax would dehydrate the tissue and skin to preserve the foot. Ensure you completely soak the feet into the mixture, leaving it for a day. After one day, take the foot out of the mixture to dry in the sun. Brush clean and add beads or any decorations you choose. Rabbit feet can also be frozen or dried for dog treats.

Tail: For centuries, the rabbit tail has been used in pollinating flowers. You achieve this by attaching the tail to a stick, rubbing it over the male and female flowers, and transferring pollen. Furthermore, the tail is used for making keychains, zipper pulls, and dog treats.

Blood: The rabbit blood is used for making blood pudding and sausage. You can use the rabbit blood to make charcuterie and to thicken sauces. The blood can be mixed with sawdust to become soil additives or mixed with water and poured around your trees, shrubs, and bulbs to fertilize them.

Liver: The liver is used for making liver pate and contains enough iron. It's also used to feed dogs, chickens, or pigs either in its cooked or raw form.

Kidney: You can either eat the kidney alone because it's nutritious and tasty or make a rabbit pot pie, stuffing, and sausage out of it. Moreover, you can feed the kidney raw to your pets.

Heart: The rabbit heart can serve as a source of trace nutrients, B vitamins, and coenzyme Q-10. You can also feed them to your pets.

Lungs: You can feed the lungs to your pigs, chickens, or pets either in its raw or cooked form.

Stomach/Pancreas: They can be used as feed for your pigs or dogs.

Uterus/Testes: They are used as raw feed for dogs, chickens, or pigs.

Rabbit Manure: It is known as the world's best fertilizer for your farm or garden. It contains about 2% nitrogen, 1% potassium, and 1% phosphorus.

Rabbit Urine: Rabbit urine mixes with water in a measurement of 10:1, fights off aphids, and fertilizes plants.

Bones: Rabbit bones make compost for bone meal fertilizer and prepare tasty rabbit stock.

Fat: It makes candles or soap and can be turned into lard or fed to chickens and pets.

Intestines: You can use the intestines to feed your pigs or dogs or dig a hole and bury them as they act as compost for your soil.

General Usage of All Parts

While the American market mainly uses the meat and dumps the rest, people from other parts of the world go beyond the meat and have found a use for every part of the rabbit. Rabbit meat gives you the protein needed for building your muscles, but the organs, when consumed, feed your organs. How? The rabbit bones, when blended, can act as a healing elixir that refreshes your digestive system. Bones and joints can be blended and made into bone broth.

The unsorted parts of rabbits that you don't need can either be fed to your pets or frozen and sold to others who may need them raw for their pets. Dogs and cats with allergies or health conditions should be fed rabbits. This is why the demand for rabbit ears, heads, organs, meat, and pelts is high.

Rabbit parts and their meat supply various prey-model raw and bone and raw food diets for dogs. With rabbits, nothing goes to waste.

The Rabbit's Fur

Every variety of rabbit has a textured fur that makes their wool or pelt production outstanding.
https://www.pexels.com/photo/selective-focus-photo-of-rabbit-2061754/

Have you ever admired your sweaters and appreciated the warm wool? Unknowingly to you, your gratitude should also be directed at the rabbit. For centuries, rabbit fur has been used for wool, which has blossomed into a significant fur trade. Every variety of rabbit has a textured fur that makes their wool or pelt production outstanding. There are different methods for removing fur from your rabbit. The first method is by burning the fur off the rabbit with fire. Another method is using hot water to peel the rabbit's fur. Thirdly, you can use the knife or without the knife technique.

Using a Knife

- Chop off the head of the rabbit or use a knife to slit its throat. It's one of the most humane ways of killing the rabbit. Another way to get the job done is by breaking the neck of the rabbit so as not to allow it to suffer.
- Just above the leg joints of the rabbit, cut a ring around each leg. At this time, the rabbit's legs should be strung on a rope. Do not cut deeply into the skin of the rabbit. Only cut enough to get to the hide.
- Make a single slice on each leg going up from the ring to the buttocks of the rabbit. It will make the skinning simpler at the end.

- Working your way from the ring cut you made earlier at the foot to the rabbit's buttocks or genital area, pull some of the hideaway. The hide should come off easily as you pull.

- Make your way through the bone of the tail by cutting through, ensuring that you do not puncture or sever the bladder in any way.

- Using both hands, begin pulling the hide from the rabbit's body. Like peeling a banana, the hide slips off easily at this point.

- Where the arm is, work your fingers into the sleeves of the hide, gently removing the arm from the hide. This could be challenging at first – but don't give up as it gets easier as you keep working your fingers through the sleeves.

- Continue pulling the hide from the upper torso to the head. Let the hide be resting at the base of the skull.

- Sever the head from the spine if you have not done it in the first steps. By this, the skin should be completely off the rabbit's remaining meat.

- Break the bones at the arm and leg with your hands, then completely remove the skin at the joint with your knife.

- Save the hides for tanning as needed while you dress and clean the meat.

Without Knife

- Place your hand around the rabbit's knee, pushing on the knee joint until it pops out of the hide, revealing the meat. You push the knee in one direction while pulling the hide in the opposite direction.

- With your finger, work your way around the leg till the hide is separated from the joint.

- While pulling the skin down, focus on pulling the knee joint upward till most skin is removed from one of the legs. This step can be likened to pulling down your pants (hide of the rabbit) and exposing your skin.

- Do the same thing to the other leg.

- Underneath the genitals, move your hands under the skin coming across the belly. Remove the skin from the belly by pulling it in.

- Put your hands on the buttocks area immediately above the tail and work under the skin to the back of the rabbit.
- Pull on the skin with both hands until it reaches the rabbit's arm.
- Break the skin between the head and the front arm with your fingers. Keep on pulling the sleeves of the hide upward, away from the arm meat.
- The spine should be cracked where it connects to the head.
- Keep the hide for tanning or other uses while you dress and clean the meat.

The Use of Hot Water

- Chop off the rabbit's head or strangle the neck to ease the pain of death.
- Put the rabbit in a bowl and pour boiled water into the bowl. Ensure that you pour the boiling water over the rabbit's body so the skin can come off easily.
- Allow the rabbit to remain in the hot water for 10 minutes. This ensures the rabbit's skin is properly soaked to help loosen it from the body.
- Start plucking off the fur from the rabbit's body. This should be easy as the water has been properly soaked into the fur.
- See to it that no fur remains and that the body is smooth by running your hands over the rabbit's body.

This technique is for those who are more interested in the meat aspect than the fur.

How to Clean Rabbit's Fur

When the skinning phase of the fur removal is over, wash off the hide in cold water to cool off right away. Do not worry about any tissue or fat left on it at this point. Your effort should be better spent on washing away the remaining blood on the skin because there is bound to be a permanent brown stain on the leather if the blood is not properly removed during this stage. If you are using soap or detergent, although not necessary, ensure traces of this cleanser are removed properly before proceeding to the next phase. Carefully extract the remaining water on the pelt once the rinsing is done.

Another way to clean the skin is with a washer. If there's a chance that bits of hair and fat will plug up the drain hose while using a washer, then avoid it and instead hand wash the pelt. It will allow you to examine the fur up close. When you're done thoroughly cleaning the hide, preserve it by drying on a stretcher, salting, drying, or freezing.

Uses of Rabbit Fur

Here are some of the uses of rabbit fur:

- Clothing
- Bedding
- Stuffing toy dolls
- For making felt

Uses of Rabbit Manure in Gardening

Can rabbit manure be used as fertilizer in the garden?

Rabbit manure is an exceptional form of manure. It has a rich, higher nutrient level, can be used fresh, and does not burn plant roots like other manure. It is just the right soil conditioner to use in any garden.

Here are some benefits of using it:

Nutrient-rich: Rabbit manure is twice as rich as chicken manure and contains four times higher the nutrient content of horse or cow manure.

Easy to work with: Rabbit manure doesn't have the same offensive odor as other manure. Being that it's in the form of little round pallets, you can handle it easily and apply it to your garden. It is also drier when compared to chicken manure.

Can be used fresh: You can apply rabbit manure directly to your garden without composting it first. Other manures, like chicken, cow, and horse dung, must be composted before being regarded as ready. If you use them fresh, they can burn your plant's roots. These manures need to be well-rotted, which takes up to three months.

Versatile: The rabbit manure pellets are used in ornamental flower beds and vegetable gardens. Furthermore, they are a rich nitrogen source to get a compost pile going and are used for up-dressing lawns.

No weed seed: Rabbit manure is usually obtained from pet rabbits not fed viable weed seed. This manure is taken from under the pet rabbit's hutches where the rabbits are kept. As sheep manure is so weedy, rabbit manure is weed-free when used in your garden. Ensure that your rabbit bedding material doesn't come close to the manure, which is why it is better to use bedding materials that are weed-seed-free.

Rabbit manure is affordable: The price tag is another wonderful benefit of using rabbit manure in gardening. You can get them locally or commercially through online retail outlets.

Rabbit manure is safe: Rabbit manure can be used around pets and plants in the house without endangering them with zoonotic diseases.

Rabbit manure is a 2-1-1 fertilizer: One main benefit of using rabbit manure is that it's a 2-1-1 fertilizer. It consists of Nitrogen, Potassium, and Phosphorus.

This makeup is just perfect for fostering the healthy growth of plants. Its plant benefits are seen from the sowing to the harvesting phase, as it supplies the needed nutrients for a resilient growth cycle.

These macronutrients are vital in rabbit manure:

- **Nitrogen:** This is needed for leafy green vegetative growth.
- **Phosphorus:** This is needed for fruiting, stem growth, and root formation.
- **Potassium:** This is needed for fruit ripening, flowering, and disease resistance.

Rabbit manure as soil conditioner: Rabbit manure is a good soil conditioner. As a source of organic matter, it enhances moisture and drainage retention and poor soil structure when buried in the soil. Due to its nutrient level, earthworms and microorganisms benefit from rabbit manure.

The Use of Rabbit Bones and Organs

The Use of Rabbit Organs

Rabbit organs are regarded as nature's nutrient-filled food. The reason is that there are many health benefits when you eat them. Rabbit liver is a reasonable size and has a mild to moderate flavor. Combined with other organs like the heart and kidney, they are tasty when fried with bacon and onions. You can grill the organs with onions and garlic, crush them into a paste, and spread them on crackers.

Here are the rabbit organs and their protein and vital nutrient content needed for your body.

- **Kidney:** It's rich in zinc, vitamins A, D, E, K, magnesium, iron, folate, and B vitamins, including B12.

- **Liver:** It's rich in potassium, zinc, vitamins A, B2, B6, B9, B12, D, C, E, calcium, magnesium, phosphorus, niacin, folate, choline, copper, and iron.

- **Heart:** It contains vitamins B6, B12, folate, iron, phosphorus, and copper. These are some of the benefits you get from the consumption of rabbit organs.

The Use of Rabbit Bones

Rabbit bones are rich in Potassium, Calcium, Magnesium, Phosphorus, and other minerals needed to develop and nourish your bones. Furthermore, rabbit bones enhance joint health.

Rabbit bone is a perfect flavor-based for broths, consommé, stock, and much more. This bone produces a silken and full-bodied broth, a good flavor enhancer for recipes. It is tasty when sipped on its own. You can boil your rabbit bones or roast them to increase their flavor. Rabbit stock, in any recipe, can take the place of water.

If you want that extra layer of savor when preparing potatoes, rice, lentils, or beans, consider including them in your dish and having them in your pantry as a major flavor enhancer.

The analogy of having your cake and eating it, in this case, is that you enjoy both the meat and its by-products because the benefits from all rabbit parts weigh more when compared to just the meat. So, next time you butcher a rabbit, know the skin, tail, head, droppings, etc., and are not just waste. They can yield more than you realize.

Bonus Chapter: Responsible Rabbit Raising: Ethics and Regulations

Congratulations! You've come a long way. You are now fully aware of what you need to know and have when raising rabbits for meat. However, there are still a few things to add - the ethics and regulations guiding the raising of rabbits.

Raising animals for food comes with a lot of responsibility. As a backyard farmer, it's up to you to ensure your rabbits live happily and healthily and are treated humanely. You'll need to make difficult decisions concerning how many litters to breed, how to dispatch the rabbits humanely, and how to sell or distribute the meat legally and ethically.

Raising rabbits for meat isn't a hobby; neither are rabbits just commodities to be sent off for food or income. It's a business that requires compassion and empathy.

The Moral Responsibility of Raising Animals for Food

Ethically, raising rabbits for meat is a big responsibility. By putting in the necessary effort to keep your animals healthy and happy and by striving to provide them with good, humane lives and deaths, you'll be able to enjoy the fruits of your labor with a clear conscience. There are some key things to keep in mind, which entail:

• Doing Your Research

Learn your rabbits' needs and make sure you can commit to meeting these needs. Proper housing, nutrition, handling, and healthcare are not optional. Therefore, research regulations regarding breeding, housing, and the regulations regarding selling meat in your area. The more you know, the better you can care for your rabbits.

Learn your rabbits' needs and make sure you can commit to meeting these needs.
https://www.pexels.com/photo/photo-of-a-woman-thinking-941555/

• Focusing on Welfare

Your rabbits should have good living conditions, opportunities for exercise, quality food, and veterinary care. Monitor them daily for signs of distress or disease and take action quickly. Handle them gently and move them calmly to avoid stress. Make sure any equipment used for their care is properly sized and maintained. Your rabbits' well-being must be the top priority.

• Committing to Responsible Harvesting

When it's time to butcher your rabbit, use the most humane methods you can, thus ensuring a quick and painless death. Have a plan in place and the proper tools for slaughtering. Remember, these animals have provided sustenance for you and your family, so they deserve your utmost respect, even at the end of their lives.

Providing Good Welfare and Humane Treatment

Providing a high standard of welfare and humane treatment for your animals is non-negotiable as a responsible rabbit farmer. Rabbits are living creatures that feel pain, fear, and distress, so they deserve your compassion.

Ensure your rabbits have spacious, well-ventilated housing that protects them from harsh weather. Provide opportunities for them to move about freely and plenty of mental stimulation. Feed them a healthy diet and give them constant access to fresh, clean water. Ensure your rabbits are monitored daily and taken to a vet as soon as needed.

Having raised these rabbits yourself, it's only right that you put them down as painlessly and quickly as possible. The most ethical option for butchering rabbits is cervical dislocation (breaking the neck), performed by a skilled operator. Some farmers prefer to hire a mobile slaughter unit to stun and kill the rabbits on-site. Whichever method you choose, make sure it causes a quick and painless death.

There are also regulations around breeding, housing, transporting, and selling rabbits and rabbit meat that you must follow. Research your city, county, and state laws to ensure you stay within legal limits for the number of does and litters permitted and requirements for selling meat. Some areas may require permits, licenses, or inspections.

As a responsible steward of animals and the environment, you must provide good welfare for the rabbits, use sustainable farming practices, and follow all regulations. By doing so, you'll feel proud of producing nutritious food in a kind and moral way.

Relevant Laws: Animal Welfare Act

Understanding legal regulations and the ethical responsibilities of raising rabbits should be a priority for backyard rabbit farmers. The Animal Welfare Act establishes rules for humane care and treatment of rabbits. Humanely treating rabbits isn't just about regulations. It's also about shaping a better world for your furry friends.

These regulations show how animals should be housed, handled, and given medical attention in laboratories or the vibrant arenas of circuses and zoos. Although the Animal Welfare Act prioritizes animals used for research, exhibition, and entertainment, it also casts a protective net over all creatures, even our beloved pets. This Act is a reminder that responsible ownership and thoughtful care extend to every corner of the animal kingdom.

The Animal Welfare Act isn't just a legal document; it's a commitment to compassion. It calls farmers to embrace empathy and kindness. As you familiarize yourself with its contents, you're committing to keeping up decent ethics and standards in the raising of rabbits.

Several states have additional laws for backyard rabbit farming. These laws cover breeding practices, selling meat, and animal cruelty. As a rabbit farmer, you have to understand these laws and regulations; carefully following them will help ensure you run an ethical, responsible operation. For example, some states prohibit the sale of uninspected meat, including rabbit meat. It's vital to check in with your local regulations.

Ethically, as a rabbit farmer, you must commit to responsible, humane farming practices that respect the rabbits' basic needs and natural behaviors. Some key principles include:

- **Providing Good Welfare**

Keep rabbits healthy, give them space to exercise, and practice positive reinforcement training.

- **Preventing Suffering**

Quickly treat injuries or illnesses, handle and transport rabbits carefully, and use humane slaughter methods.

- **Honoring Their Natural Living**

Give rabbits opportunities to socialize, forage, burrow, and play. Enrich their environment with tunnels, toys, and other stimuli.

- **Using Sustainable Practices**

Consider breeding for hardiness, mothering ability, and other useful traits. Avoid overbreeding.

By following these guidelines and maintaining high standards of care, you'll feel confident that you are acting with integrity as a backyard rabbit farmer.

Breeding Regulations

Most areas have regulations on breeding rabbits to prevent overpopulation and ensure good breeding practices. These may limit the number of litters a doe can have per year and prohibit inhumane caging conditions. Some states require breeders to be licensed and inspected.

Selling Meat Regulations

To sell rabbit meat, you must understand food production and sales regulations in your area. These typically cover:

• Licensing and Inspections

Most places require a license to sell meat and periodic inspections of your facilities.

• Processing Requirements

Meat must be processed in a licensed slaughterhouse or a government-approved personal facility. Also, follow specific rules that govern humane harvesting and handling.

• Packaging and Labeling

Meat must be properly packaged, labeled, and refrigerated or frozen to ensure safety and allow traceability. Labels provide information like weight, ingredients, producer details, and use-by date.

• Zoning Laws

These laws regulate where you can breed, raise, process, and sell rabbits in your community. Check with local authorities about requirements in your area.

Additional Considerations

Other regulations apply, such as transporting rabbits, importing new breeding stock, using pharmaceuticals, and disposing of waste. It's a good idea to check with organizations like the United States Department of Agriculture (USDA), the U.S. Food and Drug Administration (FDA), and the American Rabbit Breeders Association for the latest rules, regulations, and recommendations to follow.

Licensing Requirements for Commercial Rabbit Farms

There are certain licensing regulations you must follow as a commercial rabbit farmer. However, they vary in each country and region.

In the U.S., the United States Department of Agriculture (USDA) oversees regulations for commercial rabbit farms. Operations with over 3,000 rabbits must obtain a license, register with the USDA, and meet minimum standards of care under the Animal Welfare Act. Licensed farms are subject to unannounced inspections to check rabbits' health, housing, and humane handling.

Some of the key requirements for commercial farms include:

- Providing each rabbit with enough space to freely stand, lie, and turn around.
- Access to clean food and water daily.
- Proper heating, cooling, ventilation, and lighting systems.
- Regularly cleaning and disinfecting enclosures to keep rabbits healthy.
- Handling and harvesting rabbits according to American Meat Institute guidelines.

In addition to animal welfare regulations, there are strict requirements for selling rabbit meat for human consumption. They include:

- Meat must be processed in a licensed facility that follows proper sanitation and food safety procedures.
- Farms must keep detailed records to trace the origin and distribution of all meat sold.

As a responsible farmer, follow all regulations carefully and keep up-to-date with any changes in these regulations. Build positive relationships with inspectors and policymakers. Additionally, always remember that regulations exist to protect the welfare of your animals, the safety of consumers, and the sustainability of your farm. Following them is key to running an ethical operation.

Transporting and Handling Rabbits Legally and Ethically

Transporting and handling your rabbits in an ethical, responsible way is not only vital for their well-being but also a legal requirement. Your moral duty as a rabbit farmer is to provide humane care for your animals during all stages of their lives, including when you have to move or handle them.

When transporting your rabbits, you must follow these regulations:

- **Provide Food, Water, and Rest Periods**

In transit, rabbits must have access to food at least every 12 hours, water every six hours, and five-hour rest periods.

- **Use Proper Enclosures**

Transport cages must be constructed to protect rabbits from injury, contain waste, and allow them to stand up, lie down, and turn around.

Wire flooring is prohibited.

- **Protection from Extreme Weather**

Transport vehicles must maintain temperatures between 45 to 85 degrees Fahrenheit. Rabbits must be shaded and have fans/sprinklers in warm weather.

- **Ensure Humane Handling**

Rabbits should be handled gently. Never hold them by their ears; use grasping areas over their back and rump instead. Dropping, kicking, or throwing rabbits is strictly prohibited.

When handling and moving your rabbits on the farm, be extremely careful. Rabbits can be easily stressed, frightened, and injured if not handled properly. Move them slowly and confidently, supporting their whole body. Never chase or make sudden movements and loud noises around them.

By following these regulations and using humane practices in your operations, you'll raise happy and healthy rabbits and build a sustainable business. Your customers will appreciate knowing their meat came from animals that were well cared for.

Slaughtering Rabbits Humanely: Methods and Regulations

Once your rabbits are ready for harvesting, it's vital to do so humanely and use methods that comply with regulations.

- **Cervical Dislocation**

This is the most common method of slaughtering rabbits. It involves quickly breaking the neck to sever the spinal cord, which kills the rabbit instantly. Proper training is required to perform this technique humanely and efficiently. However, it is prohibited in some areas, so check with your local regulations.

- **Electrical Stunning**

Electrical stunning is another option. This method uses a low-voltage current to stun the rabbit before bleeding it out. Specialized equipment is required, and there are strict guidelines on voltage, amperage, and length of stun. When done properly according to the law, this method is considered humane.

- Bullet Dispatch

For small farms, bullet dispatch is allowed and considered humane when performed by a skilled marksman with the proper firearm and ammunition. However, many areas prohibit discharging firearms and have additional regulations regarding storage, licensing, noise, and liability, which must be considered.

Guidelines for Humane Slaughter

- Rendering the animal unconscious and insensible to pain immediately.
- Do not restrain the animal in a way that causes injury or pain before unconsciousness.
- Check that the animal is unconscious and does not regain consciousness before death.
- Bleed the animal as soon as it is unconscious to ensure death.
- Provide proper training to anyone performing humane slaughter methods.
- Follow all local, state, and federal laws regarding humane slaughter and food safety.

Your rabbits deserve a quick and painless end, and your customersdeserve safe, humanely produced meat. With diligence and compassion, you can achieve both.

Disposing of Rabbit Remains Properly and Legally

Disposing of your rabbits properly after slaughter is vital for legal and health reasons. As the farmer, you must handle remains correctly.

Proper Disposal Methods

The most common methods for disposing of rabbit remains are burial, incineration, and composting. Burying the remains at least two feet away from water sources is acceptable in many areas. However, some places have regulations against burying dead livestock, so check local ordinances.

Incinerating the remains in an approved incinerator is also an option. However, the equipment for this method can be expensive, and permits may be required. Composting the remains in a secure composting bin with carbon-rich brown materials like sawdust, straw, and leaves is a sustainable method, but it can take 6-12 months for remains to break down fully. The compost should not be used on food crops.

Regulations and Zoning Laws

Most areas prohibit dumping rabbit remains in landfills, waterways, and open areas. There are strict laws regarding the disposal of dead livestock to prevent the spread of diseases and pests. It's important to understand the regulations in your city or county to avoid hefty fines or legal trouble. Zoning laws may also prohibit composting and incinerating remains in residential areas. Always check with local authorities regarding which disposal methods are allowed and any permits needed on your property.

An Ethical Obligation

As a rabbit farmer, treat the remains as you would want your remains to be handled. Keeping records of disposal, composting, and incineration at high enough temperatures and properly securing remains from pests and predators are all responsible and ethical disposal practices. How you handle remains says a lot about your standard of care and respect for the animals in your charge. Do right by your rabbits even after they are gone.

There you have it - the ins and outs of responsible and regulated rabbit farming. You are responsible for your animals' welfare and must operate legally and ethically as a rabbit farmer. Provide good care, humane handling, and a sustainable living environment. Educate yourself on regulations and reflect carefully on the ethics of raising animals for food.

With diligence and compassion, you can raise rabbits responsibly without losing sight of your moral duty toward them.

With diligence and compassion, you can raise rabbits responsibly without losing sight of your moral duty toward them. Raising animals is a big responsibility, but if done correctly, it can be a rewarding experience for you and your community. The more you understand ethical farming practices, the better-equipped you are to make good decisions and set a positive example.

Conclusion

As you wrap up your learning of raising rabbits for meat, you must address a sentiment many people have grappled with - the undeniable cuteness of these furry creatures. It's completely normal to feel a twinge of hesitation when it comes to harvesting animals you've cared for. However, as you've seen throughout this guide, practical considerations and valuable insights can help you find a balance between your emotions and your goals.

Like any aspect of homesteading, Rabbit rearing comes with its own challenges and rewards. Choosing the right breed for your specific needs is the foundation of success. Be it for meat production or specific traits, understanding breed characteristics is key. Providing appropriate housing, nutrition, and medical care goes a long way in ensuring your rabbits lead healthy and productive lives. Remember that raising rabbits isn't just about physical needs - it's also about emotional well-being. Spending quality time with your rabbits, observing their behaviors, and creating a stress-free environment can contribute significantly to their overall health and contentment.

When the time comes for processing, it's essential to approach it with respect and compassion. Employing humane harvesting techniques and utilizing as much of the rabbit as possible demonstrates a commitment to ethical practices. While the path of rabbit farming for meat is undoubtedly rewarding, it's crucial to tread carefully and be aware of potential pitfalls. Maintaining a rigorous disease prevention regimen is non-negotiable. Rabbits are susceptible to various illnesses, so staying informed about potential health risks and implementing preventive measures can save you from heartache down the road.

Breeding should always be approached with a clear purpose and a commitment to improving the breed. Overbreeding or neglecting to consider genetic factors can lead to unintended health issues in future generations. Emotionally, preparing yourself for the harvest is an aspect that can't be overlooked. It's okay to have mixed feelings, but acknowledging and reconciling these emotions is essential to maintaining a healthy perspective.

Approach each step of this journey as an opportunity to learn and grow. There will be successes and challenges, each contributing to your experience and expertise. Try to create a balance between your emotional connection to the rabbits and the practical purpose they serve. Remember that raising animals for meat is a responsible choice that contributes to sustainability and self-sufficiency.

Part 2: Raising Ducks

The Ultimate Guide to Healthy Duck Keeping for Eggs, Meat, and Companionship with Tips on Choosing the Right Breed and Building the Coop for Beginners

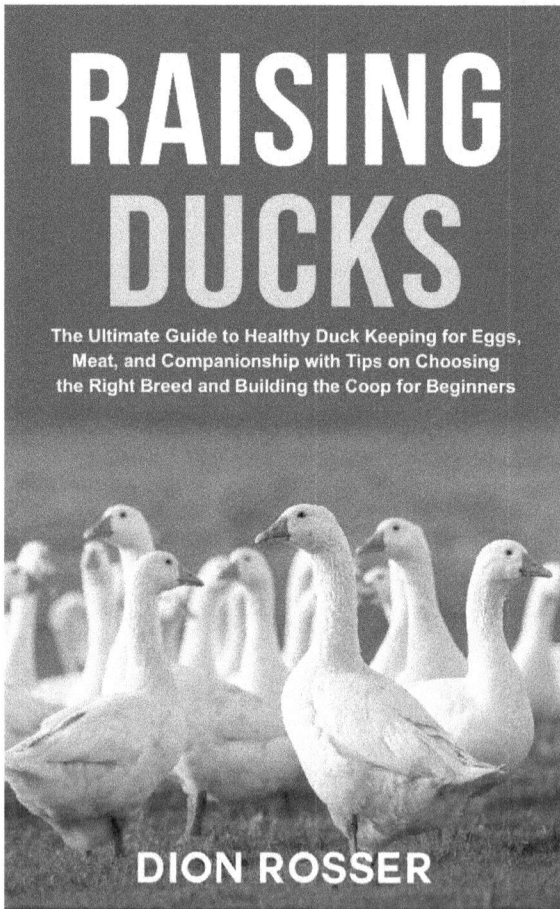

Introduction

When you imagine a typical homesteading scene, you'd probably think of a few animals, like chickens or cows, taking the spotlight. Rarely do you ever see ducks and geese. Why not, though? Just imagine happy little ducks splashing around in a little pond. Who wouldn't want that?

If you've ever dreamed of having your very own small farm, the idea of raising chickens might have crossed your mind. Chickens are commonly chosen for their eggs and companionship, but have you ever considered adding ducks to the mix? Ducks can be an exciting and rewarding addition to your farm, and they offer a unique set of benefits and joys that might surprise you.

One of the most delightful aspects of raising ducks is their egg production. Ducks are known for being excellent layers, and they can actually outperform chickens in this department. With ducks, you can have a steady supply of eggs, which are delicious and larger than chicken eggs. It's a rewarding experience that can add a unique touch to your breakfast table.

Interestingly, ducks were once poised to take the lead as the primary egg providers. However, chickens gained popularity due to their adaptability to intensive farming methods. Despite this turn, ducks remain a fantastic option for small-scale egg production, especially if you're looking for a more diverse egg selection.

Beyond the realm of eggs, ducks offer some unique advantages over chickens. One of these benefits is their natural talent for pest control. They are excellent at foraging and can keep pests in check. Unlike chickens, they won't scratch up the ground and create a mess, making them a valuable addition to your garden maintenance team. They are the low-maintenance pets of the poultry world. They're great at scavenging through the veggie patch and doing a solid job of hunting down those slimy slugs and other critters.

Caring for ducks is surprisingly straightforward, too, making it even more appealing for both beginners and experienced farmers. While a pond can be a wonderful addition to your farm, it's not an absolute requirement for raising ducks. They're content with smaller water sources, such as a kiddie pool or shallow container. This adaptability adds to their charm and makes them relatively easy to incorporate into your farm setup.

Before diving into the duck-keeping world, you should take a few practical steps. Check with your local authorities to ensure that ducks are allowed in your area. Most places are perfectly fine with a small number of ducks, but it's always a good idea to ensure you follow the rules. If you have neighbors nearby, it's also a courteous gesture to have a friendly chat with them about your plans.

Chapter 1: The Benefits of Raising Ducks

Ducks are not the first animals that come to mind when people think about raising livestock. People typically imagine raising chickens, pigs, or cows. You usually get asked if you are a dog or a cat person, never a duck person. The extent to which society interacts with ducks is limited to prints on children's pajamas, Disney cartoons, and occasionally feeding them at your local park. Aside from being ridiculously cute, these overlooked birds can be a wonderful addition to a family or homestead.

Aside from being ridiculously cute, ducks can be a wonderful addition to a family or homestead.

https://www.pexels.com/photo/yellow-ducklings-floating-on-the-sink-with-water-7697682/

Ducks come in many varieties and can be raised for several reasons, including meat, egg, and fertilizer production. Furthermore, these highly intelligent birds make great companions. Some therapists have recommended ducks as emotional support animals because they can connect with people. Humans have had a long relationship with domesticated ducks that has spanned over 500 years. For that reason alone, you will not have any problems researching what is best for the birds.

Ducks have a unique, graceful serenity that can be awe-inspiring. They are similar to dogs in that they can form meaningful attachments. One of the most common phenomena recorded among duck species when it comes to bonding is the imprinting that ducklings do at birth. If you are the first living being that a duck sees moving after it hatches, it will imprint on you and follow you around as if you were its mother. As fellow social organisms, humans share a kinship with ducks that leads to an interspecies understanding.

Ducks provide meat and eggs and can be a huge benefit to a farm ecosystem. Wandering ducks eat insects, snails, and weeds. They can then be used as part of a permaculture system that limits the use of pesticides. By minimizing pesticides in farming, ducks can help farmers transition to cleaner ways of producing food by decreasing soil and water contamination. In addition to pest control, ducks can produce natural fertilizer and compost.

Opening yourself up to the unfolding possibility of a beneficial co-existence with ducks introduces you to a new, fulfilling world. Once you learn the basics and can execute key principles of duck raising, the rewards will become increasingly apparent. Taking this leap can be one of the most enlightening decisions you ever make. Moreover, ducks are relatively low-maintenance, so you will not break your back to care for them. Low effort, coupled with innumerable benefits, is a favorable route worth exploring if you're thinking of getting a new animal.

The Pleasure of Raising Ducks

One of the stand-out aspects of raising ducks is the pleasure it can bring. Imagine the old man reading his newspaper in the park, leisurely throwing pieces of bread at passing ducks. Doesn't that image bring immediate relaxation? There's something truly grounding about interacting with ducks. The peace of mind that comes from connecting with ducks is indescribable. You will not fully understand that until you experience the miracle of raising a duck from when it was a fluffy, yellow duckling to full adulthood. The social nature of ducks allows them to form deep bonds, which are quite fulfilling for humans who share a similar drive to maintain relationships.

Ducks are beautiful to look at. These gorgeous birds come in all shapes, sizes, and colors. Sitting back and absorbing their majesty facilitates a deep sense of gratitude for the natural world. There is nothing like watching a trail of ducklings follow their mother on a pond. The way they glide on top of the water is splendidly satisfying. Ducks just seem to have an unexplainably inviting aura that you can't help but want to be around, especially when you start interacting with them regularly. You cannot fully understand what it means to raise ducks until you share a space with them.

The peace of mind that comes from connecting with ducks is indescribable.
https://unsplash.com/photos/JDzoTGToogA

If you are raising ducks for eggs and meat, the feeling of raising your produce from birth is magical. Eating your own food is worlds apart from buying plastic-wrapped food in the grocery store. There is something primal about tapping into the ancient tradition of raising domesticated animals. It is as if your ancestral memory is activated, linking you with the long lineage of people who used agriculture to propel civilization forward. As humanity moves into the next age of agriculture, where environmental concerns are taking center stage, raising ducks seems to be a way forward for conscious poultry production.

There are also financial benefits to raising ducks for eggs and meat. The duck market continues to grow, and there is room for more expansion, with turkey and chicken farming still being far ahead of duck farming. This relatively untapped market, compared to other poultry meats, has the potential to explode, especially considering the wide variety of environments in which ducks can thrive and their resilience. The satisfaction of profit can be a motivating factor to begin your duck-raising operation.

Egg and Meat Production

A primary benefit of raising ducks is the meat and eggs you can harvest. Chicken eggs are eaten in almost every household, but duck eggs are just as delicious. The beauty of ducks is that they are species that can exponentially outlay chickens. It is baffling that more farms have not embraced ducks for egg production. They do not lay daily, but you can get over 300 eggs from one duck over a year. A few ducks can completely eradicate the need for you to buy eggs from a supermarket. You'll also be able to sell the surplus. Ducks can be raised alongside chickens, so you do not have to abandon the idea of chicken farming altogether. You can introduce variety into your egg consumption by combining ducks and chickens.

Generally, ducks are healthier than chickens, so you'll have fewer disease-related issues. Ducks are also more equipped to survive in the winter due to their fat layers and thick feathers. Some species can even sleep outside in the rain and the snow. Surprisingly, ducks can even deal with hot weather better than chickens. Although chickens and ducks are both noisy, ducks tend to be quieter throughout the day. Even though they can be loud, their quacking is not consistent.

Most people consume chicken eggs, but duck eggs are better in many ways. The higher fat content in duck eggs makes for a richer flavor. Duck eggs are larger as well, so you do not only get more in terms of number, but you get greater size quantity as well. Many pastry chefs prefer duck eggs because their high-fat content can be better for baking recipes. Therefore, the superiority of duck eggs should propel you to embrace this nutritious source of protein. The noticeable switch from chicken eggs to duck eggs will have you wondering why you didn't start raising ducks ages ago.

Duck meat is a lean source of protein. Considering the obesity issues that the Western world suffers from, switching from red meat to duck meat can be life-saving. In addition to protein, duck meat is also a brilliant source of iron. Eating a serving of duck meat can provide you with half the daily iron intake. The nutrient-rich meat also contains B vitamins, which help maintain healthy hair, skin, and muscles. Duck meat has a lower fat content than chicken, so it can be useful for health-conscious people and gym-goers.

Nearly every part of the duck is edible, and the parts that can't be eaten are still useful, like the feathers or offal. Therefore, if you raise ducks for produce, nothing will go to waste. People dine on all kinds of duck meat, including the liver and gizzards. Duck liver is considered a delicacy in many parts of the world due to its unique fattiness. Their meat can be eaten with rice and vegetables for a hearty, wholesome meal. It can be prepared in various ways, including barbeque, roasting, or even in a stew.

Duck meat has more vitamins and minerals and lower cholesterol amounts than chicken, making it a healthier option. Many parts of the world have a crisis in obesity and food-related diseases like diabetes and hypertension. Exploring duck farming could be one of the solutions to addressing some of the world's nutrition issues. If duck farming is more widely embraced, the price of healthier meat will be driven down. Moreover, the larger size means that people will get more meat for their buck.

Pest Control

If you are growing produce, ducks can be a good deterrent to various kinds of pests. Seeing how they spend a significant portion of their day foraging, ducks love feeding on bugs and snails. People who raise ducks usually save a lot of money on pesticides. Even though they're very effective, pesticides, over time, can negatively impact your soil because they destroy micro-diversity that provides essential nutrients to plants. Using ducks as a form of pest control can keep your soil alive.

Asian farmers have traditionally used ducks to control the insect population in rice paddies. Species like the Indian runner have been bred to have longer limbs to cover more ground. Using your ducks for pest control can create a robust ecosystem on a large farm, smallholding, and backyard. Since they naturally forage with little intervention, ducks can basically become your partners in tending the field. With pest control ducks, your birds happily feed on insects, your plants are protected, and you'll enjoy a high-quality, organic harvest.

Ducks can be a good deterrent to various kinds of pests.
https://www.pexels.com/photo/ducklings-eating-on-ground-12295250/

Considering that climate change is propelling the globe into a new way of functioning, incorporating animals for cleaner farming methods may be necessary. The minimal harm that ducks cause and their relatively low cost of maintenance may make the bird a logical solution for embracing environmentally friendly practices in food production. Ducks can be bred for meat, which can be a useful alternative to breeding cows that generate excessive methane gas. Introducing ducks into your homestead can build a mutually beneficial ecosystem that can maintain a healthy, natural balance.

Ducks do not exclusively help with insect pests but can extend their services to include weed eradication. Ducks are both foragers and grazers. They eat weeds and small plants. If they are allowed to independently forage in your field, that will reduce the cost of their feed. The combination of weeds and insects will be a great supplement for your duck's diet. Common weed species like dandelion greens are a favorite snack for many breeds. Unlike chickens, ducks are less damaging to your plants because they eat taller shrubs and do not dig the ground up.

Small snakes, mice, and frogs are also not safe when ducks are around. These pests can wreak havoc on your crops. The hunting prowess of ducks can help maintain a low mouse population, which can contribute to avoiding infestations. Mice dig your crops out at the roots so they can threaten an entire harvest. Poisoning mice can lead to the soil getting damaged and may result in other wildlife you did not plan to kill being affected. If you have children on your property, using poison can be a catastrophic hazard. Children are curious and spend a lot of time playing outside, which means they could easily come into harmful contact with poison being used in a homestead. Using ducks for pest control can help you craft a safer environment for young ones visiting or living with you.

The Resilience of Ducks

Some cultures use ducks as a symbol of stability. This makes perfect sense when considering ducks are some of the most resilient animals. Of all the domestic poultry humans raise, ducks are the least susceptible to disease and have spectacular immunity. Therefore, whether you raise ducks for meat, eggs, or as companions, you can rest assured that they will not easily fall ill. Their strong immunities and resilience to extreme temperatures make them one of the most low-maintenance animals to keep.

In their natural environment, ducks face all kinds of external threats, including predators and the challenges of living in robust habitats. They have evolved to be strong and intelligent. Some duck species migrate over long distances and can spend extended stretches of time in the air. Furthermore, ducks are social creatures who often fight during mating seasons. The combination of duck behavior and psychology grouped with the tough environments they come from has created a lovingly resilient creature that takes no nonsense.

Ducks are an amazing starting point if you plan on catering to a diverse farm, whether for subsistence or commercial. They can be used to introduce you to the world of farming without overwhelming you because of how resilient they are. Instead of picking high-maintenance animals as your initial investment, you can begin with ducks that can provide high-end eggs and premium meat.

Ducks are not prone to diseases, so they are safe animals to keep around people and livestock. Moreover, the temperature control that makes ducks adapt to changing weather conditions makes them a brilliant option in the wake of global warming. Where many animals will perish due to the changing climate, ducks may be the best poultry option to explore to adapt to climate change. The sustainability that ducks present by laying large eggs and providing a lot of meat while playing a crucial role in the ecosystem as a predator and fertilizer makes ducks one of the most environmentally friendly livestock. Unlike cows, which take up a lot of space and produce greenhouse gases, and chickens, which often require all types of medication because they are sickly, ducks can be the sustainable meat of the future.

Duck Fertilizer and Regenerative Farming

With a mounting environmental crisis largely contributed to the livestock farming industry, ducks can present a way to embrace more environmentally friendly farming methods. Essentially, ducks are the perfect animal to create a permaculture environment with. Permaculture farming is an eco-friendly way of approaching agriculture where you construct regenerative ecosystems that work with the local fauna and flora. Pest control ducks already present a powerful permaculture asset but also provide fertilizer.

Duck waste is nitrogen-rich, giving your soil much-needed nutrients to replenish it with each harvest. Macro-nutrient nitrogen is crucial for plants to develop amino acids, the building blocks of protein that contribute to growth. Therefore, nitrogen will help your plants grow faster and bigger. Many farmers use artificial nitrogen fertilizers, which are well-formulated to help plants grow. However, these artificial fertilizers tend to focus on providing the plants with nutrients instead of replenishing the soil. Using a natural nitrogen fertilizer like duck waste is superior in the long term.

The best environment for ducks is a swampy marsh with a pond or another water source. With the ducks spending a lot of time in the water, the runoff can be built into an irrigation system with fertilizer combined with the water. A duck pond can help you save on your water bill and can be a more sustainable method of irrigating a farm. A water source with ducks creates a living system that beneficially contributes to the biodiversity of your land.

Poultry meat has also been used as a way to fertilize the soil. In many parts of the Western world, offal from poultry is not consumed or made into processed meat like nuggets or sausages. In a homestead setup, a creative way to use the offal is to bury it underneath the soil and plant on top of it. This can be used as a way to restore nutrients to the soil. Inedible parts of the duck can be used in this fertilizing process, such as its bill and feet.

Many duck breeds can be aggressive and bite people when threatened. However, some breeds are very docile. These calmer breeds are perfect as pets, especially around kids. Ducks are intelligent birds that can be taught tricks and commands. As pets, they can be trained to embrace cuddles and form a strong bond as a member of the family. Keeping one as a pet allows you to still get the benefits of fertilizer and pest control without having to slaughter the animal if you are uncomfortable with that. Whether you are a vegan or a meat-eater, ducks can be the perfect addition to your farm, yard, or smallholding.

Welcome to the World of Raising Ducks

By exploring the benefits of raising ducks, you have taken a significant step forward to uncover the layers of contentment buried underneath duck farming. As you raise your ducks from chicks to adulthood and notice their evolution, you won't be able to help but feel a certain sense of kinship with the animal. Ducks are social, intelligent, and emotional, so they are easy to establish a close relationship with. Their robust personalities and cuteness will definitely tug at your heartstrings and leave you with endless stories.

Ducks are social, intelligent, and emotional, so they are easy to establish a close relationship with.
https://www.pexels.com/photo/children-sitting-on-a-picnic-blanket-10652690/

The beauty of duck raising is in the process of having patience until your inevitable reward. The meat, eggs, or companionship you gain will prevent cognitive dissonance if you take the informed path to raising ducks. Embracing an environmentally conscious and cruelty-free method of raising ducks can present a guilt-free emotional, financial, and social fulfillment endeavor. If you are still questioning whether you should raise ducks when you have the space and time, the answer is to go for it! Ducks may be the best option for a lovable pet and livestock when you weigh the pros and cons of raising different animals. Their low-maintenance resilience makes them an awesome project to explore as an entry point into raising animals. Furthermore, their novelty and beauty will keep you entertained and wrapped around their cute little webbed feet. There has never been a better time to start raising ducks than right now, so continue reading and prepare to start this rewarding journey.

Chapter 2: Understanding Duck Behaviors

If you owned a pet before, you know how important it is to build a relationship with them. Every strong relationship requires healthy communication. Animals, however, don't communicate in the same way humans do. Due to their underdeveloped cognitive abilities and intellect, along with their less-evolved vocal cords, animals cannot speak like humans, and they never will be able to, at least not in the near future. That doesn't mean they cannot communicate, though.

Most dog owners have learned to relate different types of barks to different moods. For instance, did you know that a high-pitched whine often indicates anxiety? In cats, the kind of "meow" you hear most often (moderate pitch, medium-long cry) generally means that they want something.

Vocal communication isn't the only way to understand animals. Their behavior and actions can often be interpreted as something comprehensible. For example, you may have noticed that a cow usually lets its tail hang freely. That almost always means they feel safe. When it is stiff and tucked between its legs, it can indicate they are sick or anxious.

Do ducks, on the other hand, display communicative behavior? The good news is, they do! While you obviously won't be able to converse with them, you can certainly understand their sounds, differentiate between various noises, and comprehend their social structure to better interpret their behavior.

Duck Communication

Ducks primarily communicate vocally. Sometimes, they also use body language to express what they want. If you can pick up on their behavioral cues, you'll be well on your way to building a good rapport with them.

Vocal Communication and Unique Sounds

The most common sound a duck makes, something you had learned in elementary school, is "quack." Dogs bark, cats meow, and ducks quack. Do you know that different types of quacks mean different things? Apart from the basic quack, ducks also make a wide range of sounds, from a meek squeak to a formidable bark. As a general rule, the louder the sound, the more pressing the message.

Ducks primarily communicate vocally.

- **Quack:** Whenever you hear the loud quack sound, you can generally deduce that there are ducks nearby. Not all ducks, however, produce that sound. Only the females (hens) in Mallard ducks can generate that quintessential sound.

  Additionally, not all quacks mean the same thing. The most common interpretation of a loud quack is a mother duck calling out to its ducklings. It may also be a call for its male partner (drake) to mate. When you hear a single duck quacking in a raft of ducks, it is probably claiming a drake as its own.

Nocturnal ducks usually don't make a lot of noise. Since ducks are primarily diurnal, the nocturnal ones understand they should not disturb most of their sleeping flock with needless noise. So, when they do quack at night, it's generally a warning sign that a predator is nearby.

If pet ducks are quacking a lot around you, it may mean that they are excited to see you and eager to play with you. Don't jump into their space just yet, though. Check if they are about to lay eggs because they also tend to quack a lot.

- **Honk:** This is another frequently heard sound among ducks. Again, it is more common among the hens in many breeds. It ordinarily implies that it is trying to make its position known to its partner, especially if they are far apart in an unknown terrain (not when they are in a large crowd of ducks).

Honking while in a flock of ducks may mean the same thing as quacking - they have selected their partner. It may also mean that they have detected a predator in the vicinity (regardless of the time of day or night).

- **Hiss:** The hisses of ducks aren't normally as continuous as a snake's. They are more low-pitched and grainy, with quite a few halts in between. Both males and females of many species are known to produce this sound, especially when they are afraid of something. It's more of a whispered conversation, an apprehensive murmur, the same way you may communicate with your friends when you are threatened to stay quiet by someone.

- **Purr:** Like cats, ducks also purr, often for the same reason. Your pet duck may start purring while you are petting them, implying that they like it and want you to continue doing it.

- **Growl:** Just as your stomach growls when you're hungry, ducks growl when they want food. It's more of a low-pitch apprehensive growl than the dangerous bark of a dog. Keep a bowl of oats or birdseed ready when they make this sound.

Other unique sounds that ducks make are whistling, groaning, squeaking, croaking, sighing, and even hooting like an owl! But these are less commonly heard among domesticated ducks.

Body Language and Behavioral Cues

While sounds may be the most important form of communication with your ducks, understanding their body language comes in at a close second. They look amazingly cute when they blow bubbles in the pond, but is there a deeper meaning to the act? What do all their small behavioral cues mean, like head tilting at odd times?

- **Walking One behind the Other:** You may have noticed this often. Whenever a family of ducks walks on land, they waddle in a straight line, one behind the other. Unlike humans and many other animals, they don't usually walk side by side. In ducks, this behavior shows that they trust each other. The one leading the flock guides the rest on their way by looking straight ahead. The ducks behind the leader tend to look anywhere but the front to ensure their group isn't surprised from the sides or back.

- **Sleeping with an Open Eye:** If you own a couple of ducks and a few ducklings, you may have noticed that the adults often sleep with one eye open. They are actually asleep, but half their brain is alert with their single open eye, keeping a watch for predators.

Ducks watch out for predators while sleeping with an eye open.

- **Blowing Bubbles:** You may find it adorable when your ducks blow bubbles in the pond. They aren't exactly having fun but are removing any dirt or debris stuck in their nostrils.

- **Staring with Head Tilted**: Are your ducks giving you a thousand-yard stare with their head tilted to one side? Don't worry, they aren't scared. They are watching through their peripheral vision for either predators or food.

- **Wagging Their Tail Feathers**: Just like a dog shows excitement or happiness by wagging its tail, ducks show these emotions the same way. If they wag their tail feathers when you approach, it means they are happy to see you. On the other hand, they may simply have emerged from the pond and are drying themselves off. If that's the case, you may also find them preening the feathers on the rest of their body, distributing essential oils evenly throughout.

- **Digging Holes in Mud Puddles**: This is one of the ways in which ducks put their long beaks to good use. They have learned from experience that mud puddles usually have bugs and other insects beneath the bottom surface. They are simply foraging for food.

The Act of Imprinting

Did you know that you can make ducklings trust you without doing anything? Soon after a duckling hatches, it will learn to trust the one whom it sees the most. This process is called imprinting. It may take a few months or even years for human infants to imprint on their mothers. A duckling is quick to trust, imprinting on its mother or fellow ducklings (whoever it sees the most) as fast as within an hour!

You'll also be delighted to know that ducklings can imprint on you! Place the eggs in an incubator and wait for them to hatch. As soon as they crack open and the duckling peeks out, ensure that the first thing it sees is your face. Stay with it for an hour or two, and let it keep seeing you. Pet, caress, or handle it, and even talk to it if you can.

A duckling is quick to trust, imprinting on its mother or fellow ducklings (whoever it sees the most) as fast as within an hour!

https://unsplash.com/photos/8hbJLsUHULE

You won't know right away if the duckling has imprinted on you. When it grows up and starts exhibiting any of the excitement behaviors mentioned above when you approach (like wagging its tail feathers), then you can be somewhat certain that you succeeded. Does the duck let you easily handle and care for it when it's sick? Only then can you be absolutely sure that it trusts you!

Social Structure of Duck Flocks

Ducks have a social structure in their flocks. It helps them reduce internal conflicts and live in harmony with each other. Even if they do reach a conflict, the flock leader ensures that it is resolved or that a compromise is reached.

Social Hierarchy

The social hierarchy or pecking order in ducks is loosely based on physical appearance. The stronger the duck appears to be, the higher it will be placed. Age doesn't really factor in. A duckling who has just matured into a healthy duck with graceful features may start leading a pack of other, more experienced ducks.

A pecking order is more commonly observed in hens. Did you know that a flock leader always lays its eggs first? The other ducks have to hold until the hens higher on the social ladder have dropped their eggs in the nest. Sometimes, a better-organized flock may stand on each other with the leader at the top and lay their eggs one by one (top first). That way, if a predator is lurking around, they can protect their eggs together. Also, it may be the lead hen's way to stress its leadership.

Drakes also have a social hierarchy, which can be observed when they are mating. If you have several drakes but just one hen, you may have noticed that the ducks mate individually. The first drake to mate is usually the strongest one and the leader of the flock.

Ducks have a pecking order while eating, too. The next time that you leave a bowl of feed near their nesting area, wait a while and observe them eat. They will rarely ever huddle around the bowl together. The first few ducks that come to feed will be the leaders of the flock, followed by the next in the hierarchy.

If you observe them every day, you will notice that the last (lowest order) batch of ducks never goes hungry. That is because ducks can assess the quantity of feed very well and distribute it evenly among the entire flock.

Flirting and Mating

It's a joy to watch ducks flirt with each other. You may even learn a thing or two! The courting habits of ducks are no different to humans. Have you noticed drakes emerge from the water, dripping wet, flaunting their plush-soaked feathers by ruffling them in the sun? How often have you seen men do the same thing after emerging from a public pool, ruffling their hair while flaunting their bodies?

The hens usually nod their heads in approval. When they also flatten themselves, belly down, in the water, it is an invitation for the drake to mount her. If the female doesn't approve of the male, the latter may have a few other flirting techniques, like scooping up water in its beak and flipping it at the hen.

Ducks are able to mate in the water as well as on land. They feel more comfortable in the water because the buoyancy lets the hen spread herself more freely. Granted, the water's instability may make them lose their balance while mounting, but the drake holds on to the neck of the hen with its beak to avoid falling off.

Ducks are able to mate in the water as well as on land.
https://pixabay.com/photos/ducks-birds-animals-mating-6384735/

The act of mating itself is not as graceful as you would think it to be. The uninitiated may feel like your ducks are fighting, with the drake trying to pin down the hen. At times, multiple drakes may converge on a single hen, and neither of them gets hurt in the process. It's just how their mating ritual is. They aren't monogamous.

The males are the most amorous of the lot. A drake will have one female, which it prizes above others. It will feed, care for, and even spend the most time with her. That won't hold it back from mating with other nearby hens. The drakes are like the kings and emperors of yore, who married the queen of their heart but also kept several mistresses.

On the other hand, a female duck has only one male romantic interest at a time (it may have several in its lifetime). However, other drakes are free to mate with it if they want, even if the hen has no desire for them. Consent doesn't really feature in their relationship, but don't feel too bad. That's the way they live.

Common Behavioral Problems and Their Solutions

Ducks are living, breathing beings with health and behavioral issues like any other animal. Due to their relatively advanced intelligence and high emotional quotient, they also tend to face psychological problems. They usually don't keep things bottled up inside. Their problems are often reflected in their behavior. The most common ones include,

Weird Vocals

Is your waterfowl making a weird sound? Try to relate it to any of the vocals mentioned in the "Duck Communication" section. If it's neither the fairly common honk nor the immensely rare hoot, the duck may be trying to express a problem in its health, like an infection. Is the sound low-pitched or hoarse? It may be trying to alert the presence of a predator. Either way, you need to take it to a veterinarian to ensure it doesn't spread to the other ducks if it's an infection.

Low Egg Frequency or Quality

Does your mother duck rarely lay any eggs (say, no more than once or twice a week)? Regardless of the frequency, are the eggs laid of poor quality (look rotten or bad)? It is a common problem during winter, which can be easily avoided by increasing the amount of their food. Ducks tend to spend more energy in the cold weather to keep their body temperature in check. Hence, they need more food in especially harsh winters to keep their energy levels up.

Overeating

Humans tend to overeat during stressful times. Ducks, on the other hand, may overeat because of humans. It really depends on the diet you are giving them. If you are including a lot of bread and junk food in their diet, it may cause several health issues. Stick with grains or oats. If you don't have them stocked, let them forage for themselves for a while. Their health problems may just vanish into thin air. If they persist, visit a vet.

Causing Self-Harm

Does your fowl often pick its feathers? Does it scratch itself to the point of bloodying its skin? Does it tend to cause harm to itself in any way? They are displaying antisocial behavior due to increased stress. Are you keeping the duck isolated from its family? Do you own just one duck? Ducks are social animals by nature, and when they don't get a chance to interact with their fellow ducks or ducklings, they may start to harm themselves. Unite it with its family or bring new ducks into the fold.

If the duck inflicts self-harm while present in a group, it may be infected with a parasite. Take it to a vet right away.

Repetitive Actions

Is your duck exhibiting repetitive behavior, like waddling back and forth or circling in the same small area? This is another indication of stress. It may be due to isolation from the flock. Alternatively, are your ducks confined in a congested space? They are used to, or have evolved to, live free and unhindered in the wild. They need a lot of space to ensure the stability of their mental health.

Let them roam around in your backyard from time to time. Ducks are called waterfowl for a reason. If you don't have a private pool or pond, lead them to a pool in the neighborhood (provided the owner agrees to let the ducks jump in!) Lack of sexual activity could also be a major cause of stress, so ensure each drake has a hen to mate with.

Chapter 3: Choosing the Right Breed of Duck

Ducks make fantastic additions to your farm and can thrive independently and alongside chickens. If you've ever raised poultry before, you're likely aware of the joy it brings, and raising ducks offers an equally rewarding experience. Ducks take pleasure in exploring the farm or yard, much like chickens, and they share the appetite for feasting on insects, including larger ones like slugs and grasshoppers, which sets them apart from their feathered counterparts.

The world of ducks boasts a diverse array of breeds, and for those new to duck-keeping, selecting the right breed can seem daunting. In this chapter, we aim to simplify the process by providing you with insights into various duck breeds. We'll delve into their distinctive characteristics, specific requirements, and the unique contributions they bring to your farm. Furthermore, we'll delve into the strengths and weaknesses of each breed, including their temperament, egg production capabilities, size, foraging prowess, and adaptability to varying climatic conditions. This comprehensive guide will equip you with the knowledge you need to make informed decisions when it comes to choosing and caring for your ducks.

The Various Duck Breeds

Finding the ideal duck breed begins with a clear understanding of your specific goals and needs. Your choice of duck breed should align with the purpose you have in mind. Here are some crucial questions to guide your decision-making:

1. **Determine Your Purpose**: What role do you envision for your ducks?

   - Are you primarily interested in egg production?

   - Do you seek a duck breed renowned for its meat yield?

   - Are you in search of charming backyard companions capable of pest control?

   - Are you interested in ducks known for their foraging skills, sociable nature, or calm demeanor?

   - Is heritage breed conservation a priority, leading you to consider breeds classified as threatened or critical?

2. **Consider Additional Factors**: Beyond your primary purpose, think about other factors that matter to you:

   - **Size**: Larger breeds may offer better protection against aerial predators.

   - **Aesthetic Appeal**: Are you looking for visually striking duck breeds?

   - **Mothering Ability**: If breeding is part of your plan, consider a breed that excels in nurturing ducklings.

3. **Assess Your Commitment**: Recognize the level of effort you're willing to invest in your chosen duck breed's care and maintenance:

   - Are you prepared to gather eggs regularly?

   - Can you handle the needs of larger breeds, including assisting with hatching if necessary?

   - If you prefer chatty ducks, are you ready for continuous communication with them?

Once you've determined what you can offer and your primary objectives, you'll be better equipped to identify the most suitable duck breed for your farm or lifestyle. Keep in mind that the best breed for you is the one that aligns with your specific requirements.

Top Duck Breeds
Indian Runner

The Indian Runner boasts one of the most unique builds in the duck world. It is an unusual-looking breed of domestic duck.

The Indian Runner boasts one of the most unique builds in the duck world.

Bjoern Clauss, CC BY-SA 2.5 <https://creativecommons.org/licenses/by-sa/2.5>, via Wikimedia Commons: https://commons.wikimedia.org/wiki/File:Runner-ducks.jpg

Characteristics

They belong to the lightweight category of domestic duck breed. They have long necks, slender heads, and slim bodies. Their long neck has earned them the description of a "wine bottle." Due to their longer neck, their eyes are set high, with a straight bill. Their legs are positioned way behind the back of their body, which is different from other duck breeds. An Indian Runner can run and at the same time shuffle quickly due to the position of their legs and the shape of their bodies.

When agitated, they stand fully erect. Normally, they have a 45 - 75% degree of carriage above eye view. From the crown of their head to their tail tip, the small female's height is 20 to 26 inches, while the taller male's height is about 70 inches.

The drake's tail tip is a bit curled, while that of the ducks is flat. You might be unable to tell the difference between the drakes and the duck until both mature.

When compared to other breeds, they have 14 color varieties, including Trout and white, Fawn, Mallard, Silver, Apricot Dusky, Chocolate, Cumberland Blue, Black, Apricot Trout, Blue, Blue Trout, Blue Dusky, Light brown, Dark brown. Eight varieties of runners are registered with the American Standard of Perfection, and they include gray, Cumberland blue, chocolate, buff, black, penciled, white, and the original Fawn and white.

The ducks have a body weight averaging 1.4 to 2kg, while the drake's body weight is averaging 1.6 to 2.3 kg.

Needs

Indian Runners don't need special dietary or living quarters. They only need a conducive space with a sleeping spot, clean water, clean bedding, and regular poultry bird food to keep them happy and healthy. Unlike other duck breeds, Indian Runners require less water. A water tub to dunk their head into is enough.

Unique Value

Indian Runners are wonderful foragers and major egg producers. They are also good for controlling pests.

Temperament

Indian Runners are docile and friendly. They get along well with other pets like dogs and cats. However, they become very aggressive while protecting their little ones or when they sense danger and feel threatened.

Egg Production

Indian runners are well-known for their ability to lay eggs. They lay over 300 to 350 eggs yearly. At the least, they lay 5 to 6 eggs a week. The eggs Indian Runners lay are large and pastel green in color. They are sought after due to their distinct flavor, making them excellent for baking.

Foraging Ability

Indian Runners are popular independent foragers who enjoy hunting for hidden snacks like insects, snails, slugs, and seeds.

Adaptability

They can adapt to all climates, even those extremely hot or cold. Their egg production might reduce during cold weather, but it will not cease. No matter the hardiness of the ducks, precautions should be taken during the harsh climate to ensure they have access to clean water and shade. Their coop should be properly ventilated at all times, too.

Khaki Campbell

If you are looking for a beginner-friendly duck capable of laying more eggs, then Khaki Campbell is your go-to duck. Khaki Campbell originated from England and was introduced to the world around 1898. Mrs. Adele Campbell of Uley, Gloucestershire, England, developed the Khaki Campbell ducks. Being a poultry keeper, she purchased an Indian Runner, which she crossbred with the Rouen and other wild ducks, resulting in khaki Campbell.

If you are looking for a beginner-friendly duck capable of laying more eggs, then Khaki Campbell is your go-to duck.

Characteristics

Mistaking a typical Mallard duck for a Khaki Campbell duck is very easy. A Khaki Campbell has a long neck with a boat-shaped body. Its feathers and wings have a light or dark khaki color. Depending on the duck's gender, a Khaki Campbell duck can have a black or green bill with dark orange to brown legs. The female Khaki Campbell ducks often have dark features like khaki feathers, while the male counterparts have light features like light khaki wings and feathers.

On a Khaki Campbell, you will notice curls of white on the duck's chest. These ducks have beautiful feathers, and the color range of their skin is from white to a bit yellow, based on the types of feed given to them. Khaki Campbell ducks are known to be medium-sized ducks, with their weights never exceeding 4.5 lbs. for both the males and the females.

The female average weight is from 3.5 to 4 lbs., while the male average is from 4 to 4.5 lbs. In height, both are averaging from 1.5 to 2 feet.

Needs

Khaki Campbell ducks do not require a special diet. As ducklings, you can feed them non-medicinal chick starter feeds. Once they are 3 months old, you can feed them game birds, chicken feed, or waterfowl. Due to a potential choking hazard risk, scratch-style feed is not recommended for ducks. Nevertheless, pellet varieties of chicken feed and crumble are known for feeding domestic breeds of ducks. If the Khaki Campbell duck is in a coop or duck house, endeavor to feed them grit to enable them to properly digest their food without any issues.

Unique Value

Most people raise Khaki Campbell ducks mainly for their egg-laying ability. It is a breed that fits duck commercial farming based on its popularity as one of the best egg-laying ducks. This breed is also used for meat production. They are exceptional foragers and would eat anything from various invertebrate pests they encounter. They are your backyard and garden rangers who would take care of anything that might sting or cause itching to your family or threaten your crops.

Temperament

The Khaki Campbell ducks are strong, robust, and active. They are calm, friendly, and passive when raised by hands until maturity, irrespective of the misconception of them being skittish or of flighty behavior.

Egg Production

This duck's area of strength is that it can lay up to 300 eggs per year, 4 to 6 medium-sized white eggs per week. It is highly regarded for its dual purpose because of its ability to produce both eggs and meat. They start laying eggs as early as 21 weeks old.

Foraging Ability

This breed has excellent foraging ability and should be given room to roam. They don't do well when confined.

Adaptability

Khaki Campbell ducks can survive in every climate due to their cold, hardy nature.

Pekin Ducks

Although old, American Pekins is a well-known dual-purpose duck known for its meat and egg production. This breed is now in many countries and is one of the most known breeds for commercial purposes. The main reason it's called American Pekin is to differentiate it from the German Pekin.

American Pekins is a well-known dual-purpose duck known for its meat and egg production.

Djm-leighpark, CC BY-SA 4.0 <https://creativecommons.org/licenses/by-sa/4.0>, via Wikimedia Commons: https://commons.wikimedia.org/wiki/File:Trio_of_Pekin_or_similar_ducks_on_Fishbourne_Mill_Pond,_West_Sussex_(2240o).jpg

Characteristics

The American Pekin duck is beautiful to behold. They have long necks and bodies, yellow skin, and large breasts. The color of their feathers is either creamy white or white. Their bill is yellow, and their legs are orange-yellow or reddish. Their rump is overturned, and their posture is more vertical than dabbing ducks. When you closely observe these ducks, you'll see their eyes are grayish-blue colored irises. The weight of a Pekin duck is from 8 to 12 pounds.

Needs

Pekins need a clean space to shield them from rain and wind, a fence to keep them contained, and access to water and food. Due to its limited flight ability, the fence should be low. Pekins enjoy both natural and commercial food. If you give them free-range access, they can eat their favorite food from nature. In commercial production farming, commercial feed is usually fed to these ducks. The ducklings can be fed with chick starter feed.

Unique Value

Perkins performs dual-purpose functions. They are raised for meat production in America. The duck meat consumed in the United States is 95% Perkins duck. This breed is also perfect for egg production. It can give you an average of 200 white-colored eggs yearly.

Temperament

Perkins ducks are intelligent, non-aggressive, and friendly. Those who raise them either as pets or egg birds can pet them from time to time. Pekins like to be touched. You can lay them upside down in your lap and stroke their bellies.

Egg Production

Pekins can average 200 to 300 large eggs yearly. When a Pekin hen is 5 to 6 months old, she begins to lay eggs.

Meat Production

This is the primary reason Pekin ducks are reared in America. 95% of the duck meat consumed by the average American is Perkin duck meat. The meat is rich in protein and has a tasty flavor. It doesn't have the texture or greasy taste of other duck meat. At 6 weeks old, a Pekin, weighing around 6 pounds, is ready to be butchered. A Jumbo Pekin's average weight is around 9 to 11 pounds when they reach 12 weeks old. The increased weight associated with Pekin ducks is one of the main reasons they are reared for their meat.

Foraging Ability

They're excellent foragers as they can forage for most of their diet.

Adaptability

Due to its hardy nature and strong and resilient immune system, Pekin ducks can adjust to any climate.

Muscovy Ducks

The Muscovy duck is a well-known big domestic duck breed that originated in North America and is found in states like Massachusetts, Florida, and Hawaii. This is the only domesticated breed not obtained from the Mallard duck.

The Muscovy duck is a well-known big domestic duck breed.
Fredricx, CC BY-SA 4.0 <https://creativecommons.org/licenses/by-sa/4.0>, via Wikimedia Commons: https://commons.wikimedia.org/wiki/File:Muscovy_ducks_outside.jpg

Characteristics

Muscovy duck is a unique breed that can be spotted miles away because of their distinctive look. Their bodies are heavy, thick, and strong. Their feet are wide-set, long webbed that makes them waddle. Muscovy ducks, like turkeys and gobbles, have bumpy skin-like markings on their face. Furthermore, their bill is long and sloping in nature.

The male and the female Muscovy grow to the same height. Their height is around 26 to 33 inches, while their wingspan grows from 54 to 60 inches based on the duck's height.

The Muscovy duck has a fluctuating weight, mostly in adulthood, based on their habitat and the food they consume. The average body weight of the drake is around 4.6 to 6.8kg. Although the big, domesticated drakes weigh up to 8kg, the ducks weigh 5kg.

Needs

Your ducks need to be sheltered from predators and other elements. Ensure the shelter is well-ventilated to avoid any respiratory issues and large enough for them to roam freely.

Muscovy ducks enjoy roosting and perching, so make perches using wood or metal placed at various heights in the shelter. Put a nest box in the shelter to allow female Muscovy ducks to lay their eggs. Since they need access to water, they build their shelter close to a water source, a pond, a large dish of water, or a shallow pool.

Feed them with commercial feed and supplement their diet with fruits, vegetables, and greens.

Unique Value

Based on their versatile nature, Muscovy ducks have benefits ranging from pets to food production and agricultural uses. They are reared mainly due to their meat and egg production. This duck is handy when controlling pests, composting, and being kept as pets.

Temperament

Muscovy ducks are gentle and friendly to have as pets. They welcome the attention of both their owners and guests because they are not easily afraid or threatened by the presence of people.

Egg Production

These ducks are not a major producer of eggs. They can lay over 80 to 120 eggs yearly and hatch and raise four sets of Muscovy ducklings yearly. Their eggs are much larger than those of other breeds and tastier than chickens', making them a more favored choice for cooking.

Meat Production

This is where Muscovy ducks thrive the most. Their meat is very tasty and tender compared to veal and beef. Their breast meat is lean, and their skin contains less fat underneath it compared to other duck breeds.

Foraging Ability

Their foraging ability is top-notch. They can easily hunt for food when given the room, making them great for pest control.

Adaptability

This duck can adjust to any climate based on its hardy nature and ability to fly.

Aylesbury Ducks

The Aylesbury duck is a pink duck whose primary purpose is meat production. It is considered a backyard/ornamental bird due to its beautiful appearance and friendly nature. It is a domestic breed from the United Kingdom. The duck was developed in Aylesbury in Buckinghamshire, England, in the early 18th century.

The Aylesbury duck is considered a backyard/ornamental bird due to its beautiful appearance and friendly nature.

Characteristics

Aylesbury is a big-sized duck breed. It has white skin and a thick white plumage that uniquely sets it apart from other domestic breeds. They have a horizontal carriage and a long body. Their keel is straight, deep, and almost touching the ground. The Aylesbury has a long, straight, pinkish-white bill with legs and feet colored orange. It has a boat-shaped body due to the placement of its legs midway to the body, and it stands upside down parallel to the ground. They have swan-like long and thin necks with dark grayish-blue colored eyes.

Aylesbury ducks are of two types: the exhibition type and the utility type. The exhibition type has a deep keel, which makes it hard to mate naturally. The utility has a smaller keel, allowing them to mate successfully naturally. The average weight of the Aylesbury drake is about 5 kg, while the duck averages 4.5kg.

Needs

Aylesbury needs feed with many grains like barley, wheat, etc., and protein feeds such as fish meal. Additionally, it needs clean water, so put a container in their enclosure. Better still, you can let them free-range around ponds and other water sources as they enjoy foliage.

Unique Value

Aylesbury is primarily raised for meat production. Aylesbury are great companions if you are looking for a friendly and easy-to-manage pet. They are great for small spaces and can bring beauty to your garden. These ducks will make you smile by entertaining you with how they constantly chase each other. These ducks protect against mosquitoes as they excel at controlling mosquitoes in your backyard or garden. With their ranger ability to look for slugs, your backyard would be free of any stinging insects.

Temperament

Aylesbury is friendly and docile towards humans. They are sociable and enjoy being in groups. Feel free to let them socialize with other ducks in your home, but be careful of the drakes. They are capable of mating with any duck they encounter.

Egg Production

Aylesbury can produce eggs, but it's not something you should count on if you are into commercial farming. Within a year, a female's average egg production is 35 to 125 eggs.

Meat Production

Aylesbury is mainly known for its meat production, so they are reared as utility birds.

Foraging Ability

Aylesbury has an excellent foraging ability and, when allowed to roam, can cater for some of their feeds.

Adaptability

Aylesbury duck has a strong tolerance for all climates.

With these breeds in mind, choosing the right one for you should not be hard.

Chapter 4: Housing Your Ducks

If you're just starting out with raising ducks, creating the ideal housing and environment for them can seem daunting. Though relatively easy animals to handle and maintain, ducks have specific needs for shelter and protection. They require safe spaces to be shielded from potential predators and unpredictable weather. Whether you house your ducks within an existing structure or construct a dedicated duck coop, the key is providing them with security, nourishment, and enough space to move freely.

This chapter will guide you through the process of designing, building, and maintaining a duck coop or enclosure that caters to your ducks' specific needs. You'll find valuable insights into constructing a secure and cozy space for your feathered companions, with tips on design variations inspired by popular structures. By the end of this chapter, you'll be well-prepared to create a habitat that protects your ducks and enhances their overall quality of life, ensuring they thrive in their new environment. Whether you're a novice duck owner or an experienced enthusiast, the knowledge you gain here will contribute to the well-being and happiness of your beloved duck flock.

Ducks, though relatively easy animals to handle and maintain, do have specific needs for shelter and protection.

You don't necessarily need a full-scale barn to ensure safe and comfortable housing for your ducks. In fact, you can create a suitable living area on your property or even use a separate building for just this purpose. Whether you opt for a do-it-yourself (DIY) approach to building a duck coop or consider purchasing a pre-made enclosure, there are several critical elements to take into account before making a decision.

1. **DIY vs. Pre-made**: Decide whether you want to build your duck coop from scratch or purchase a pre-made one. DIY coops offer customization options but require more time and effort. Pre-made coops can save you time but may have limitations in terms of size and design.

2. **Location:** Choose a suitable location for your duck coop. It should be well-drained to prevent waterlogging, easily accessible for feeding and cleaning, and ideally situated to provide protection from prevailing winds.

3. **Size and Design**: Consider the size of your duck flock when designing or choosing a coop. Ducks need ample space to move

around, so ensure the coop is roomy enough to accommodate them comfortably. A good rule of thumb is to allow at least 3-4 square feet of indoor space per duck.

4. **Materials:** Whether you're building or buying, select materials that are durable, weather-resistant, and easy to clean. Common choices include wood, plastic, and metal. Ensure the coop materials are safe for your ducks, as some treated wood or paints can be toxic.

5. **Roofing and Flooring:** Use a sturdy roofing material to keep your ducks dry, and consider adding an overhang to protect the coop's entrance from rain. A solid, easy-to-clean surface like concrete or wooden slats works well for flooring. Provide plenty of bedding material for insulation and comfort.

6. **Ventilation:** Proper ventilation is crucial to maintain air quality and prevent moisture buildup, which can lead to respiratory issues. Install vents and windows with screens to ensure good airflow.

7. **Security:** Ducks are vulnerable to predators like raccoons and weasels. Ensure your coop has secure locks and sturdy wire mesh on windows and openings to prevent unauthorized access.

8. **Accessibility:** Make sure the coop is designed for easy access for cleaning, egg collection, and daily care. Adequate access doors and ramps for ducks to move in and out are essential.

9. **Insulation**: Depending on your climate, you may need to insulate the coop to regulate temperature extremes. This is especially important if you live in an area with cold winters.

10. **Cost and Budget:** Consider your budget when planning your coop. DIY projects may be more cost-effective but require more time and effort. Pre-made coops offer convenience but may be pricier.

11. **Future Expansion**: If you plan to increase your duck flock in the future, design or select a coop that can accommodate growth without major modifications.

What Do You Need for Your Duck Coop?

With ducks, build a cage firm enough to keep them secluded in an area with enough water and straw under their feet, and they're good to go. When building a structure, use a wooden box or an old dog house at least 3 feet high and 4 feet in length and width.

The coops should be placed directly on the ground with enough room for future adjustments. In addition, ask yourself relevant questions like "How many ducks do I plan on raising?" and "For what reason exactly?" People raise ducks for many reasons, such as meat, eggs, and pets. No matter your purpose, you should consider the following elements.

1. Ventilation Is Vital

Ducks engage in certain habits that may lead to a less-than-pristine living environment. They tend to sleep on the ground, often leaving behind a trail of droppings right where they rest. Additionally, ducks typically make a beeline for their nests after a swim, not minding their damp and sometimes muddy state. It's crucial to understand these behaviors and take steps to maintain a healthy and hygienic living space for your ducks.

Proper ventilation is very important when customizing your ducks' shelter.
https://www.pexels.com/photo/dirty-equipment-industrial-plant-industry-416423/

When providing shelter for your ducks, consider the following:

- **Proper Ventilation**: Adequate ventilation is essential to prevent the buildup of moisture in their sleeping areas, which can lead to health issues. Make sure that your coop has well-placed vents to allow for the circulation of fresh air. Positioning the ventilation area closer to the roofline helps maintain good air quality.

- **Coop Height**: Ideally, the coop's height should be around 3 feet to accommodate your ducks comfortably. This height provides ample space and allows for better air circulation.

By guaranteeing these aspects, you give your ducks access to clean and uncontaminated air, promoting their well-being and reducing the risk of illness.

2. Protection Against Predators

Ducks are vulnerable to a variety of predators, ranging from wild dogs, raccoons, foxes, wolves, bears, hawks, wild cats, and cougars to even domestic dogs. These opportunistic predators are drawn to the delectable taste of ducks, making it crucial to take proactive measures to safeguard your feathered friends.

Here are effective strategies to shield your ducks from potential threats:

- **Reinforce Enclosures**: Create fortified enclosures with sturdy walls and doors equipped with multiple latches. This provides an initial layer of protection. In rural settings with minimal predator presence, you can also consider using chicken wire as a cost-effective alternative, although it may be less secure.

- **Urban and Forested Areas**: If you're raising ducks in an urban or forested environment where predators are more prevalent, invest in a robust protection system. Consider wired electric fences or heavy-duty fencing to deter potential threats. Additionally, employing a livestock guarding dog can significantly enhance the security of your duck flock.

- **Scale According to Needs**: Tailor your protection measures to the scale of your duck-raising operation. If you have just one duck or a small number, strategically place your coop where you can easily access it. While this may seem simpler, it's crucial to prioritize safety even with a modest duck population.

Remember, the safety of your ducks is paramount, and the level of protection you choose should align with the potential risks in your specific environment. By implementing these strategies, you can guarantee the well-being of your ducks and enjoy peace of mind as you raise them.

3. Bedding and Nesting

When preparing a nesting area for your ducks, you need to select the right bedding materials for their comfort and hygiene. Opt for dry, organic materials with excellent absorbent qualities. Suitable choices include:

- Straw
- Hay
- Wood shavings
- Cedar shavings
- Shredded papers
- Chopped leaves
- Pine needles

When preparing a nesting area for your ducks, you need to select the right bedding materials for their comfort and hygiene.

Make sure you have an ample supply of these materials on hand for easy replacement whenever your ducks make a mess. While changing the bedding daily is unnecessary, it's advisable to remove soiled bedding every few days.

Instead of discarding the used bedding, consider repurposing it as compost for your garden. This eco-friendly practice reduces waste and enriches your garden soil with valuable nutrients, ultimately benefiting your ducks and plants.

By following these guidelines, you can create a clean and cozy nesting environment for your ducks, all while promoting sustainability in your gardening practices.

4. Good Location

One of the key advantages of having a portable and mobile coop is the ease with which you can disassemble and reassemble it when needed for location changes. Coop mobility becomes essential when adapting to changing weather conditions and ensuring the well-being of your ducks.

Consider these scenarios where portable coops shine:

- **Weather Adaptation:** In the face of changing weather patterns, such as excessive sun or harsh winter conditions, you can effortlessly relocate your coop. For example, during scorching summers, moving the coop to a shadier, cooler area with access to fresh water ensures your ducks stay comfortable. Conversely, relocating to a warmer spot in colder months provides essential protection.

- **Preventing Dead Spots:** Regularly shifting the coop prevents your backyard or garden from developing unsightly dead spots. This mobility fosters healthier soil quality and contributes to a more vibrant environment for your ducks to thrive.

The continuous adaptability of a portable coop not only enhances your ducks' living conditions but also positively impacts the soil quality, creating an ideal setting for their growth and well-being.

5. Spacing per Duck

If you plan on raising more than one duck, you'll have to be certain each one has at least 3-5 square feet in the coop. Multiply 3-5 square feet by the number of ducks you plan on raising and see how much spacing you will need.

6. Build a Larger Duck Coop than Needed

Constructing a duck coop doesn't have to be an expensive endeavor. In fact, you can make the most out of leftover materials from previous projects to create a thrifty yet efficient duck shelter. Here's how to optimize your coop-building process:

- **Resourceful Recycling:** Gather any leftover scraps from past repairs or projects in your yard. These seemingly insignificant leftovers can be ingeniously combined to craft a functional duck coop. This not only saves on costs but also reduces waste.

- **Plan for Expansion:** Embrace the idea of potential growth in your duck-raising venture. Consider building a larger coop than currently needed, with expansion in mind. While it may seem unconventional, trust in the process and anticipate future changes. Begin with a minimum of 4 square feet of flooring per duck, and plan to expand to 12 square feet as your flock grows.

This approach caters to your present requirements and positions you favorably if you decide to accommodate additional ducks later on.

By adopting these strategies, you can construct a cost-effective duck coop that serves your immediate needs while allowing room for future expansion while making the most of available resources.

Unique Coop Designs for Your Ducks

If you're planning to raise multiple ducks, it's essential to consider the right coop structures to accommodate them comfortably. Whether you choose to make them yourself or order pre-made coops, adequate space is key. Here are some innovative duck coop designs to inspire your duck-keeping venture:

1. Tyrant Quacker Box

- The Tyrant coop can house up to six ducks, offering mobility with its wheels and making location changes hassle-free.
- This design features a nesting box measuring 3 feet high, 3 feet wide, and 4 feet long, topped with a removable, waterproof green roof.
- The coop incorporates approximately 1-inch galvanized wire mesh to deter predators, which is especially effective in safeguarding ducklings.
- The Tyrant Quacker Box proves to be an efficient choice for duck protection and care.

2. Artisan Urban Coop

- Designed with urban settings in mind, this mobile coop features wheels for easy maneuverability.
- The coop structure utilizes chicken wire for ventilation and includes a cozy, dog-sized house for your ducks' comfort and safety.
- Its mobility allows you to shift it effortlessly, preserving grass and enhancing soil health.

DIY Artisan Coop

If you're inclined to build your own Artisan-style coop, here's a basic guide:

Materials required: Plywood, nails, screws, wood glue, metal sheets for roofing, hinges, latches, wire mesh, hardware cloth, paint or sealant, pressured timber, and roosting bars.

1. Begin by planning the coop's size based on your duck count, allocating approximately 3-4 square feet per duck.

2. Create a foundation using pressured 2×4 wood, building a balanced, square, rectangular frame aligned with your layout plan.

3. Establish vertical supports for the coop walls and attach the rectangular frame securely.

4. Frame the top and bottom of the walls using horizontal 2x4s, considering space for doors, vents, and windows.

5. Construct a simple yet effective roof frame from 2×4s, attaching it to the coop walls.

6. Add nesting boxes to the roof using plywood, each with a 12' width and 12' length, and a sloped roof for drainage.

7. Install a 2×2 roosting bar above the floor inside the coop.

8. Create openings for ventilation and windows in the walls, covering them with mesh wires or hardware cloth for predator protection.

9. Install a convenient access door and a ramp for ducks to enter and exit the coop.

10. Cover the roof frame with waterproof and weather-resistant metal sheets or shingles.

11. Apply non-toxic, mild paint to the exterior to safeguard your coop from the elements.

3. Promise Land Duck Wagon

The Promise Land Wagon is a spacious and portable coop solution for your ducks, designed to be pulled by a small tractor or an ATV.

Its metal roofing incorporates a gutter system to efficiently collect and store water, with a substantial 65-gallon capacity.

This coop grants your ducks the freedom to roam your property without the constant search for water sources.

4. Green Willows

The Green Willows A-framed coop offers versatility to accommodate various flock sizes.

You can easily customize its dimensions to suit your needs. For example, an 8x6x6-foot structure suits around 10 ducks, while expanding to 10x8x7 feet provides ample space for about 15 ducks.

This design is straightforward to build and mobile, allowing your ducks to move freely. It offers ample nesting, bedding, feeding, and watering areas.

Building a DIY Green Willows Design
Materials

- Wired mesh
- Bamboo sticks or thatch for roofing
- Recycled hinges and latches
- Sustainable wood
- Saw, drills, hammer, and nails
- Natural paints or sealants
- Measuring tape

Procedure
Construction Steps:

1. Begin by sketching a layout that incorporates gentle curves and a natural, harmonious aesthetic with your surroundings. Utilize recycled materials and sustainable wood to minimize costs.

2. Craft a curved or undulating base frame resembling the graceful flow of a willow tree. Ensure all points are balanced and aligned.

3. Add vertical wooden supports to the base frame, securing them with screws or nails, leaving space for windows and ventilation.

4. Install the roofing using bamboo sticks or thatched panels for their safety, sustainability, and natural look.

5. Create a central circular area within the coop for nesting and bedding, constructing sustainable wooden nesting boxes with sloped roofs to facilitate egg collection.

6. Cover ventilation openings with wire mesh or eco-friendly fencing to ensure proper airflow while keeping predators at bay.

7. Build a ramp with reclaimed or sustainable wood, attaching it securely to the coop's entrance to help ducks easily access it. Test the ramp for safety.

8. Apply natural paints or sealants to protect the wood from the elements. Line the coop's interior with straw and hay for bedding.

9. Place your Green Willows coop in a suitable spot within your backyard or chosen location.

10. Regularly inspect the coop for repairs or upgrades and maintain its natural ambiance to extend its lifespan.

5. Hill Homestead With Flat Mobile Coop

The Hill Homestead design offers a rectangular and practical mobile coop solution if you're budget-conscious.

Outfitted with chicken wire mesh, metal roofing, and a single or double-hinged door, this coop is compact and easy to move without needing a tractor or ATV.

These innovative coop designs provide excellent options for raising ducks, catering to various needs, budgets, and preferences. Choose the one that best suits your situation and confidently embark on your duck-raising adventure.

Tips on Maintaining a Safe and Clean Coop

Keeping your ducklings healthy and secure while maintaining their living environment is paramount. Proper hygiene helps prevent fungal infections and diseases, and safeguarding them from predators is equally essential. To ensure your duck-raising venture thrives, consider these professional tips:

1. Start Small for a Smooth Beginning

- If you're new to duck farming, begin with a small flock, perhaps five ducklings, to familiarize yourself with the basics. Once you gain confidence and expertise, you can gradually expand your flock.

- Carefully plan and research the resources, time commitment, and potential challenges involved, such as theft, predators, and regulatory permits. Starting small also minimizes the cleanup effort required for larger flocks.

2. Social Ducks Are Happy Ducks

- Ducks are social creatures, much like chickens. If you're new to duck-keeping, having at least two ducklings to provide companionship is advisable.

- Consider getting ducks of the same sex (pairs of females or males) to prevent potential breeding complications.

3. No-Tip Bowls for Food and Water

- Ducks love water and tend to be a bit clumsy with their sideways-set eyes. Use no-tip bowls for food and water to minimize spills and mess.

- Craft or purchase no-tip water containers that keep their bowls consistently filled, ensuring a steady supply of clean water day and night.

4. Choose Low Dust Bedding

- Opt for low-dust wood shavings like Aspen as bedding for your ducklings' brooder. These shavings are odor-free, highly absorbent, soft, and free from pest contaminants.

- Using low-dust bedding ensures clean air quality in the coop and reduces the need for frequent cleaning due to dust buildup.

5. Use Pellet Food and Keep It Separate

- Pelletized food is an excellent option for duck feed, offering three variations: Mash (unprocessed feed), Pellets (steamed and formed kibbles), and Crumbles (derived from pellets with a powdery texture).

- Pellets are ideal, especially if you want to minimize waste and mess. Separate the feed and water bowls to prevent contamination and maintain cleanliness.

6. Maintain Predator Defense

- Ducks are appealing prey for predators, especially in rural areas. Implement robust predator defense methods to safeguard your flock.

- Regularly inspect and reinforce coop security to deter potential threats.

In this comprehensive guide, you've discovered DIY coop designs, maintenance tips, and essential insights for raising happy and healthy ducks. By prioritizing hygiene, safety, and the well-being of your ducks, you'll embark on a rewarding journey of duck farming with confidence.

Chapter 5: Duck Nutrition: What to Feed Them

Like humans, ducks have nutritional needs for every stage of their lives. For instance, ducklings require higher protein levels than adult ducks because they are still developing and growing.

Ducks' dietary needs also differ depending on their purpose. If you raise them for meat production, they will need a different diet from the ones you are raising for eggs.

Whether your ducks are loving pets or a source of food, they need a balanced diet to live a long and healthy life.

This chapter explains in detail duck nutrition, various feeding types and their pros and cons, risks of malnutrition, and safe treats to give your ducks.

Ducklings require higher protein levels than adult ducks because they are still developing and growing.

https://unsplash.com/photos/cyG0m2JpL8Y

Nutritional Needs for Every Stage of the Duck's Life

You should feed your ducks food appropriate for their age and needs. Like babies, there are certain types of food that ducklings won't handle until they are fully grown.

Three Weeks and Younger

Ducks three weeks and younger should eat crumbles that are high in protein. They need plenty of protein (about 18-20%) at this stage of their life because they are still developing. However, you shouldn't chicken-feed them as this type doesn't have enough vitamin B3 and other nutrients ducks crucially need at this young age.

Three to Twenty Weeks

At this stage, feed your ducks high-quality food that aids growth. The food should either be for ducks or young chickens. Since their needs are changing, lower protein levels to 15%.

Twenty Weeks and Older

Now that your duck is a full-grown adult, it will require a different diet. Feed them breeder food or a high-quality layer that is suitable for adult chickens or ducks. There are many options to choose from, but mixed grains and pellets are your best options. Suppose you are raising ducks for their eggs. In that case, you must pay extra attention to their diet because nutritional deficiencies can cause various diseases and render their eggs inedible. They will usually need a daily dose of calcium to produce strong eggs. Try shell grit since it contains about 38% calcium.

You can also give them a commercial diet with the appropriate amount of fruits and vegetables.

Now that you understand how to feed your duck based on age, you need to learn how to provide a balanced diet filled with the necessary proteins, vitamins, and minerals.

Proteins

When people hear the word protein, the first thing that often comes to mind is meat, poultry, or fish. However, ducks don't require the same type of proteins that humans or animals consume. They just need the amino acids that exist in proteins. Amino acids are necessary for ducks' growth and can protect their health in every stage of their lives.

Similar to humans, ducks require about twenty-two types of amino acids every day. Some of them are produced naturally inside of their bodies, while they can only get the others from eating food high in proteins.

To guarantee that your duck will grow properly and healthily, feed it food containing these amino acids.

Methionine

Methionine is one of the most essential amino acids you should include in your ducks' diet. You can find it in cereal grains, Brazilian nuts, sesame seeds, eggs, and fish. There is also a supplement called DL-methionine that you can give to your ducks in organic feed. However, if you don't want to give your duck chemicals and prefer to stick to a natural diet, only focus on foods that contain methionine rather than giving them supplements.

Give ducklings up to two weeks old about 0.70% of methionine. During their growing period, reduce it to 0.55, and then 50% during their breeding age.

Lysine

According to a study published by Dr. Ariane Helmbrecht, a specialist in animal nutrition, ducks need at least 1% of lysine amino acid for their development. When they are three weeks old or less, they require high levels of lysine to speed up their growth and reduce the risk of any health issues. After this period, they will only need between 0.7 and 0.95%. Lysine is usually found in soybeans, fish, hemp seeds, pumpkin seeds, shellfish, eggs, and snails.

Arginine

If you raise ducks for their meat, feed them food containing arginine. This amino acid can increase their weight without needing to feed them extra meals. You can find arginine in dairy products, brown rice, buckwheat, cereals, corn, oats, sunflower seeds, and sesame seeds. Meat ducks only require 1% of arginine.

Vitamins and Minerals

Ducks need to be exposed to the sun regularly to get their vitamin D needs. However, some areas don't usually get enough sunlight, especially during the winter. In this case, you must provide your duck with Vitamin D, specifically Vitamin D3, through food or supplements. A Vitamin D deficiency can lead to many health issues like weak eggshells and bones. If your duck has low levels of phosphorus or calcium, you can make it up by increasing their Vitamin D intake. Kelp contains high levels of Vitamin D, so include it in your duck's diet.

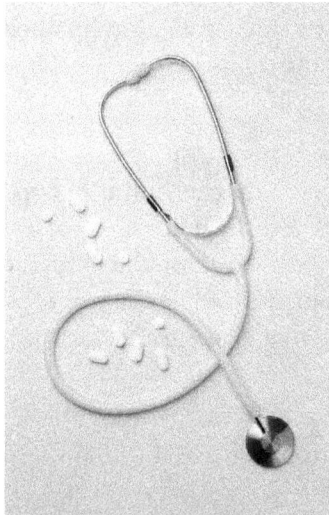

Just like humans, ducks need their vitamins in order to grow and be healthy.
https://www.pexels.com/photo/yellow-stethoscope-and-medicines-on-pink-background-4047077/

Your ducks also need Vitamin A and calcium for their health and development. You can usually find them in formulated foods, vegetables, and greens. Weak eggshells are a clear sign of calcium deficiency. Monitoring your duck's eggs is necessary as they can tell you so much about their health. Calcium supplements will strengthen the ducks' bones and eggshells and protect them against osteoporosis and reproductive diseases.

Laying ducks need more calcium than meat ducks. If you want your duck to lay healthy eggs, feed them food with high calcium levels, like sunflower seeds.

Your duck will also require a regular intake of Vitamin E to improve their immune system. Include greens in their diet; this is much easier if you have a yard or a small garden.

Grains are a great source of Vitamin E, Vitamin B, and Phosphorus as well. Give your ducks whole grains, corn, or oats, but avoid getting them wet, as they can be poisonous for them.

Niacin, commonly known as Vitamin B3, is vital for your duck's health. In fact, they require a much higher level of niacin in their diet than chicken. Therefore, chicken feed for your ducks isn't recommended since they won't get adequate Vitamin B3.

Niacin can improve the ducks' blood circulation, nervous system, digestion, feathers, and skin health. It is necessary to feed your duck food rich in niacin from a very young age regularly. Vitamin B3 converts carbohydrates, fats, and other nutrients into energy. This process can lower cholesterol, protect them from diabetes, and improve their muscle tone.

Ducklings require a daily dose of 10 mg of niacin, and adult ducks require 12.5 mg per day. Food containing niacin includes sunflower seeds, pumpkin, feeder fish, sardines, salmon, tuna fish, whole wheat, peanuts, sweet potatoes, and peas.

Niacin deficiency is extremely serious and can lead to many health issues like diarrhea, loss of appetite, slow growth, joint and leg problems that can affect movements, and in some severe cases, it can be fatal.

Ducks require other types of minerals in their diet to improve their growth rate, increase their weight, and aid in producing high-quality eggs.

• Selenium

• Iron

• Manganese

• Zinc

- Copper
- Potassium
- Sodium
- Cobalt
- Iodine
- Magnesium
- Chlorine

Many types of food are rich in minerals, like widgeon grass, southern naiad, pondweed, milfoil, coontail, wild celery, wild rice, and other aquatic plants.

Clean Water

All living creatures need clean and fresh water to survive, and ducks are no different. Your ducks should have access to clean water all day. Whether you are raising them for companionship, their eggs, or meat, they mustn't go for more than eight hours without water. Lack of water can be dangerous for their health. It can affect their mental and physical health as they can exhibit signs of stress, anxiety, and destructive behavior.

Ducks and ducklings don't only need water for drinking, but they love to bathe and go swimming as well. Think of your duck as a little child who will get excited whenever it sees water and wants to jump in right away. However, don't let your duckling go swimming until it reaches two weeks old.

You can place an artificial pond for them in your backyard so they can have access to swimming and exercise all day. Keep the pool clean by regularly removing dead plants and leaves and draining the water.

The Pros and Cons of Various Feeding Types

There are various ways to feed your ducks. Choose the method you are comfortable with that fits your environment and financial situation. This part of the chapter focuses on the pros and cons of the most common feeding types.

Foraging

Foraging or free range allows your ducks to explore their environment and find their own food. Some people believe that it is unhealthy to feed your duck because you won't be able to provide them with all the nutrients they need. Foraging comes easy for them since it's in their nature to search and hunt for food. They will get their nutritional needs from flies, worms, beetles, slugs, and snails. In fact, a duck will happily choose a bug over regular feeding or any other source of protein you give them.

Foraging or free range allows your ducks to explore their environment and find their own food.
https://pixabay.com/photos/duck-mallard-bird-nature-wildlife-899078/

Pros of Foraging

Gives Them a Chance to Exercise

Ducks are extroverts. They like to be in groups to socialize and quack about different topics. Foraging allows them to spend time with each other to exercise, bond, and look for food. They can move around and stay active instead of being confined in a small space. Ducks prefer looking for food over being served every meal. When you let them forage, you allow them to be in their natural habitat. On the other hand, ducks in confined spaces are usually stressed and can suffer from various health issues. Ducks that forage are much healthier and happier.

Protects Them against Diseases

Active ducks are less likely to get sick. When ducks are in confined places, they don't get enough exercise and are usually in close proximity to other ducks, leading them to contract diseases from each other. Foraging also exposes ducks to sunlight and fresh air, which is necessary for their well-being.

Provides Them with More Protein Intake

Although commercial feed can provide ducks with protein, a foraging diet is much richer in proteins that they can easily find in bugs and other insects.

Better for the Environment

Unlike commercial feed that uses fungicides, herbicides, pesticides, and harmful chemicals, foraging is better for the environment. Foraging is a natural method that can keep your ducks healthy and protect green areas in your city.

Protects Grass and Lawn

Foraging protects your lawn and grass from damage. When ducks have little space to roam, they will only walk on the lawn and kill your grass. If you have many ducks, their waste can also ruin your plants. When you allow them to forage, they can move around in large spaces, so their waste won't be an issue since it will be distributed in various areas, and they won't focus on a small part of the land.

Controls Insects

Since your ducks will eat the bugs in your backyard or garden, the number of insects will decrease drastically. They can also hunt rats and mice to reduce the pest problem in your home.

Saves Money

Instead of spending money on commercial feed, let your ducks forage for their food. You'll end up saving a lot of money.

It Is More Humane

Animals and birds shouldn't be confined in small spaces. They should have ample space in nature to move freely. Foraging is more humane because it puts the ducks in their natural habitat, making them healthier, happier, and less stressed and bored. Confinement can cause ducks to exhibit unhealthy behavior, like biting their skin and plucking their feathers.

Cons of Foraging

Predators

Foraging exposes ducks to predators like dogs, foxes, and owls. Placing a fence and net isn't always helpful. So, if you live in an area populated with wild animals, consider another feeding type.

Escaping

If something happens that frightens or stresses your duck, it may run off and never come back! They can also fly away, making it hard for you to catch them. If you can't keep your ducks safe, foraging may not be a good idea.

Damage Flowers

Ducks will eat any type of plant in your backyard, including flowers. So, if you have a flower garden, they will destroy it.

Home-Mixed Feed vs. Commercial Feed

Commercial feed offers your duck store-made food, usually made of by-products and cereal grains. Home-mixed is mixing various types of food to prepare a nutritional meal for your ducks. Most people struggle with choosing between home-mixed feed and commercial feed. You certainly want to keep your ducks healthy, but there are many things you should consider.

Pros of Home-Mixed Feed

- More beneficial than commercial feed
- Filled with more nutrients
- Cheaper than commercial feed
- Doesn't contain chemicals

Cons of Home-Mixed Feed

- Time-consuming
- If you aren't aware of the proper nutrients, you won't be able to prepare a healthy meal and cause malnutrition.

Pros of Commercial Feed

- Easy and cheap (Read the label to make sure it has everything your duck needs)
- High levels of protein
- Contains minerals and vitamins

Cons of Commercial Feed

- May not always meet your duck's nutritional needs
- Can contain chemicals or additives
- More expensive than foraging and home-mixed feed

• Contains pesticides that can cause cancer

The Risk of Malnutrition in Ducks

Ducks can suffer from malnutrition if they don't get the necessary nutrients. In fact, it is the leading cause of death among ducks. Malnutrition can affect their immune system and cause various health problems.

Feather Plucking

Feather plucking is often a clear sign that a duck is suffering from malnutrition. They are either not getting enough protein or getting too much fat and carbohydrates. If ducks aren't getting enough minerals or vitamins, they will pluck or chew their feathers. In some severe cases, they can chew off all of them. Featherless ducks are prone to infections and skin ulcerations.

Diarrhea or Constipation

Malnutrition can cause diarrhea, constipation, or even both at the same time. Their stools can be soft and more frequent, or you will notice small dry droppings here and there. Diarrhea and constipation are clear signs that you need to change your diet. Contact your vet right away so they can run the necessary tests and recommend the appropriate nutrients or supplements.

Egg Binding

Egg binding occurs when the duck struggles with passing its eggs. Sometimes, they can be so large that they get stuck. This can cause serious infections or even death.

Lethargy

Similar to humans, if ducks are suffering from malnutrition, they will feel lethargic and sleepy. Remember, ducks are active creatures that don't like to sit still and enjoy socializing. So, if you notice their behavior changing, it is a sign that something isn't right.

Preventing Malnutrition in Ducks

Malnutrition can easily be avoided with these simple tips.

Feed Your Duck a Balanced Diet

A balanced diet is the best remedy against malnutrition. Feed your duck with the necessary fats, proteins, minerals, and vitamins. Give them the appropriate percentage for their age and needs. If you change their diet, but they aren't getting better, consult their vet, as they can recommend a better diet or supplements.

Clean Everything

Make sure to clean their artificial pond and to only provide them with fresh water. Their food should also be clean and fresh.

Provide Them with Physical Activity

Ducks aren't stagnant creatures. Provide them with the opportunity and space to exercise. If you live in a safe area, leave your ducks to forage for their food.

Avoid Junk Food

Junk food can affect your ducks' health and cause obesity and heart attacks. Avoid feeding them any food that doesn't have nutritional value, like crackers and bread.

Safe and Unsafe Treats and Foraging Plants

Express your love to your ducks by feeding them delicious treats. However, you should make sure that you only give them safe plants.

Safe Treats

- Uncooked worms
- Mealworms
- Dandelion
- Clover
- Fresh herbs
- Leafy greens like lettuce
- Grains
- Nuts
- Grass cuttings
- Cooked beans
- Cooked eggs
- Eggshells

Unsafe Treats

- Spinach
- Raw eggs
- Raw meat

- Bread
- Chocolate
- Caffeine
- Salty food
- Dried beans
- Green Potatoes
- Green tomatoes
- Raw potatoes
- Garlic
- Onions
- Rhubarb leaves
- Fruit seeds and pits

Safe Foraging Plants

- Wild violets
- Wild strawberries
- Smartweed
- Purslane
- Purple deadnettle
- Plantain
- Oxalis
- Mugwort
- Fat hen
- Dandelion
- Creeping Charlie
- Clover
- Avocado
- Tobacco
- Oat
- Potatoes
- Philodendron
- Nightshade
- Milkweed

- Foxglove
- Elephant ear
- Eggplant
- Coffee Bean
- Calla Lily
- Buttercup
- Black locust
- Avocado

Unsafe Forage Plants

- Oleander
- Oak trees
- Mountain Laurel
- Larkspur
- Clematis
- Castor bean
- Boxwood
- Ivy
- Pokeweed
- Honeysuckle
- Bleeding heart
- Azalea
- Yew
- Wisteria
- Rhododendron
- Daffodil
- Iris
- Buttercup
- Tulips
- Sweet peas
- Poppies
- Lupine
- Poppies

Raising ducks is a considerable responsibility. They are living creatures that require constant care and attention. You should learn their nutritional requirements based on their age and needs. This is specifically necessary if you are going to feed them home-mixed food. For commercial feed, read the label on the food packages to check if they have sufficient proteins, minerals, and vitamins.

Ducks love water. They either drink it or swim in it. Place an artificial water pond or even a small swimming pool for your birds to swim and exercise. They should also have a large space because birds suffer in confinement. They can use this space to forage their food and get sunlight and fresh air. Foraging is one of the cheapest, healthiest, and most humane feeding types. However, if you don't have the time or space, you can choose between home-mixed or commercial feed.

Monitor your ducks' weight and habits to ensure they don't suffer from malnutrition. Prepare balanced meals and give them the necessary supplements to protect their health and prevent the risk of weak eggs or diseases. Finally, learn about safe and unsafe plants and treats to avoid accidents that can risk your bird's life.

Chapter 6: Duck Health and Wellness

Ducks' graceful movements and charming appearance are delightful additions to ponds, farms, and homesteads. Providing them with essential healthcare and wellness is crucial to improving their overall well-being, longevity, and productivity. While ducks may appear hardy and self-sufficient, they are not immune to the challenges that affect all living creatures. They can succumb to diseases, parasitic infections, and environmental stressors that compromise their health and well-being. Neglecting their healthcare can lead to suffering and reduced productivity.

The essence of this chapter lies in recognizing the vital role of proper duck healthcare and wellness. By gaining fundamental insights into their unique needs and vulnerabilities, you'll be equipped to be a responsible and caring steward of your feathered friends. This knowledge will enhance the ducks' overall well-being and longevity and maximize their productivity, whether through healthier egg-laying or pest control.

Common Health Issues

Respiratory Infections

Ducks suffering from respiratory infections can show signs of sneezing, nasal discharge, coughing, and experience difficulty breathing. With certain respiratory infections, you might even hear wheezing when they breathe in certain respiratory infections.

Make sure that their coop has proper ventilation to prevent moisture buildup. Besides cleaning the housing, keep the environment clean and dry, avoiding overcrowding. If the ducks have access to an artificial water body, clean it regularly to prevent the development of water-borne diseases like avian cholera. Provide ducks with a well-balanced diet to support their immune system.

Botulism

Ducks suffering from this toxin-releasing infection show signs of paralysis, weakness, and drooping of the neck, head, and wings. The Clostridium botulinum bacteria thrive in stagnant and contaminated water sources. Keeping the water source clean and uncontaminated will significantly prevent the development of botulism-causing bacteria. The containers that provide fresh drinking water should also be cleaned regularly to further inhibit disease-causing microorganisms' development. In severe cases, isolate the affected birds and provide supportive care if necessary.

Avian Influenza (Bird Flu)

Bird flu or avian influenza in ducks starts with clear signs of respiratory distress and reduced egg production. As the infection progresses, ducks might exhibit a swollen head and, in severe infections, can even face sudden death. Avian influenza is a viral infection. Therefore, it's imperative to follow biosecurity measures. Limit the ducks' contact with other wild animals or birds, keep the premises clean, and follow vaccination protocols implemented by relevant authorities. You should also notify your veterinarian and report the disease to authorities, as this highly contagious disease can spread like wildfire. Lastly, don't forget to minimize contact with other bird species, as most wild and poultry birds are potential carriers.

Duck Viral Enteritis (Duck Plague)

Ducks infected with duck viral enteritis will experience loss of appetite, an increase in depression, and greenish or blood-tinged diarrhea. In severe cases, viral enteritis can even result in sudden death. For the flock's safety, isolate new ducks before integrating them. Maintain a clean and sanitized environment to minimize the risk of disease transmission.

Parasitic Infections

Ducks suffering from parasitic infections exhibit mild to severe feather loss, significant weight loss, decreased egg production, and visible parasites on the feathers and skin. Regularly cleaning and disinfecting the duck housing is essential. Other preventative measures include giving the ducks access to dust where they can roll to naturally keep the parasites under control. You should also administer appropriate deworming treatments after consultation and supervision with the veterinarian.

Duck Cholera

Your ducks will start showing signs of lethargy, lose their appetite, and experience difficulty in breathing. Slowly, the joints will become swollen with progressively worsening symptoms. Maintaining a clean environment, like keeping their housing, water sources, and feeding areas clean, can keep duck cholera at bay. Veteran duck farmers suggest avoiding overcrowding and providing a well-balanced diet to strengthen the immune system and metabolic processes.

Aspergillosis

Ducks will show labored breathing, coughing, persistent nasal discharge, lethargy, and limited movement in this lung infection. The primary cause of aspergillosis development is high humidity. Keeping the housing ventilated, clean, and dry will prevent the growth of harmful fungi and other microorganisms.

Egg Binding

This is a common egg-laying-associated condition occurring in female ducks. The eggs fail to release through the oviduct in the female's reproductive system, pass through the maturation process, and complete the egg-laying process within the standard time. Ducks with this problem will show signs of lethargy and will make several visits to the nest due to abdominal straining.

Providing a calcium-rich diet is crucial to promote eggshell formation. Also, make comfortable nesting boxes and bedding and monitor the egg-laying behavior and frequency, as this information can be provided to the veterinarian for better diagnosis and treatment.

Leg and Foot Problems (Bumblefoot)

The most common limb-related problem with ducks is the bumblefoot. It's an abscess that forms at any area on the bird's footpad. It will start as a small, red, and inflamed bump that can deepen and increase in size. These bumps can also turn into lesions or sores, depending on their immunity levels and the cleanliness of the premises. The most evident sign of bumblefoot is the growth of these bumps or sores, which should be monitored and treated immediately.

If several ducks are affected by these bumps, immediately clean the flooring, replace the bedding, reduce humidity through adequate ventilation, and feed them a balanced diet to keep their immunity levels at optimum. However, if you are not seeing effective results, contacting a veterinarian and following their guideline can prevent this bacteria from spreading further.

Newcastle Disease

This is a highly contagious viral disease common in ducks, chickens, turkeys, and pigeons. It causes frequent sneezing, coughing, problems with digestion and production of greenish diarrhea, and neurological signs like paralysis and twisting of the neck. The female ducks affected by this viral disease also have reduced egg production.

Newcastle disease is a viral infection that spreads from the affected ducks to the rest of the flock. Therefore, always practice stringent biosecurity methods like quarantine and isolation to prevent disease spread. Lab tests can be done to confirm it before vaccinating.

Mycoplasma Induced Infections

Mycoplasma gallisepticum is a microorganism that causes chronic respiratory diseases in ducks and poultry birds. When fully developed, the disease causes decreased egg laying, persistent nasal discharge, coughing, sneezing, and inflammation around the eyes (conjunctivitis). Like any other disease, maintaining good hygiene can reduce the disease spread.

Duck Hepatitis

This is an acute viral infection primarily affecting ducklings under six weeks old. Duck viral hepatitis (DVH) has three subtypes and does not affect older birds. The ducks affected by the viral infection show jaundice (yellowing of eyes and skin beneath the fur), lethargy, and decreased food intake. DVH spreads in unsanitary environments, especially from water sources and already infected ducks. Isolating the infected ducks and minimizing overcrowding is crucial to minimizing the spread.

Regular monitoring is necessary as it can reveal signs of illness, behavioral changes, or any unusual symptoms. You can share the insights with a certified veterinarian for a better diagnosis and treatment. Following the required husbandry practices like keeping the housing clean, providing a balanced diet, and implementing biosecurity measures can significantly decrease the risk of several health issues and diseases.

Parasitic Infections (Internal and External)

While there are several parasitic infections, most show common signs of weight loss, decreased appetite, feather loss, and visible parasites on the feathers and skin in severe cases. Most parasitic infections can be decreased by improving sanitation, providing dust baths, deworming, and treating external parasites.

Parasitic Protozoa (Coccidiosis)

Coccidiosis is a parasitic disease found commonly in wild and farm ducks. This parasite reaches the duck's gut through contaminated food. The parasite lives within the gut, feeding and reproducing. Coccidiosis causes decreased appetite, lethargy, bloody diarrhea, and significant weight loss. It's best to consult a veterinarian for an appropriate treatment immediately. To minimize the outbreak, follow a regular cleaning schedule like disinfecting and cleaning the housing and providing them with fresh, healthy food.

Early detection, prompt intervention, and collaboration with a qualified avian veterinarian are essential for accurate diagnosis and effective treatment of these diseases and parasites. Implementing a comprehensive health management plan, including biosecurity measures, proper nutrition, and regular monitoring, will contribute to the overall well-being of your duck flock.

Maintaining Hygiene

Maintaining adequate hygiene is necessary to prevent disease spread and improve the health and wellness of your duck's flock. Here are some practices you can incorporate into the duck hygiene management routine.

Sanitize Living Areas

Disinfecting the housing, perches, feeding utensils, and nearby water sources. Don't let waste accumulate in a specific area. Replace wet or unsanitary bedding and leftover food to prevent the development of harmful microorganisms and pest attraction. Before using disinfectants or cleaners, make sure that the substances are safe for ducks.

Provide Clean Water

Providing fresh and clean water for both drinking and bathing is vital. Regularly changing the water prevents the growth of bacteria, contamination, and disease transmission, and it is free from contaminants like feces, droppings, and debris.

Proper Waste Management

Designate a water disposal area away from the duck living spaces where you can compost the leftover food or dispose of the waste while reducing disease transmission.

Implement Quarantine Procedures

As many viral infections are transmitted by contact with already infected ducks, implementing strict quarantine and monitoring practices can guarantee your flock's health. Whenever you want to add more ducks to the flock, quarantine them to prevent the introduction of potential diseases. Monitoring the quarantined ducks for any signs of illness is done during quarantine.

Biosecurity Measures

When introducing ducks to a new place, follow biosecurity measures and limit visitor interactions, especially with people in contact with other poultry birds like turkeys and chickens. Likewise, limit their access to wild birds as they are potential carriers and transmitters of avian diseases. If your ducks suffer from an ongoing disease, outbreak, or infection, make sure that all visitors and caretakers use sanitized clothing and feasible footwear and follow biosecurity protocols to contain the disease's spread.

Maintain Dry Conditions

Keep the housing area dry and prevent standing water through regular cleaning. Keeping the area ventilated, especially in humid conditions, will limit the growth of bacteria.

Dust Baths

Dust bathing is a natural method practiced by ducks to remove external parasites, keep their feathers clean, and prevent the development of skin-related diseases.

Foot and Hand Hygiene

Besides caring for the duck flock, maintain adequate foot and hand hygiene after handling and feeding them. Use foot baths with added disinfectant when entering and exiting the duck area to minimize disease transmission.

Provide a Balanced Diet

To keep your ducks healthy and thriving, adequate nutrition must be provided to strengthen the immune system, increase metabolism, and keep the body ready to fight an infection or a disease.

Education and Training

The diseases and conditions shared here are the most common ones, but there are several other diseases you should be familiar with as a caretaker. Reading more, joining duck farming communities, talking with duck farmers, and sharing your passion can increase disease knowledge. For better understanding, you can discuss the symptoms, preventative measures, and treatment protocol with other duck farmers.

Attending workshops and discussing disease-related issues with an avian veterinarian will also enhance your ability to promptly address these diseases and infections. Integrating these hygiene practices into your duck management routine allows you to create a clean and disease-resistant environment and contribute to the health and longevity of your flock.

Seeking Veterinary Help

It's necessary to understand when to seek veterinary assistance. You need to look out for several red flags as they indicate an underlying illness, disease, or a medical condition that might require veterinarian assistance.

Unusual Behavior

Ducks' behavior changes significantly when they suffer from a disease or a medical condition. They will become less active, avoid interaction, isolate themselves, or exhibit aggressive behavior. These are some signs that something might be wrong with their health. Consulting a veterinarian can help identify and address any underlying issues causing these behavior changes.

Respiratory Infection Symptoms

Ducks, like all animals, can suffer from respiratory infections. It could indicate respiratory issues if you notice symptoms such as frequent sneezing, coughing, labored breathing, nasal discharge, or unusual sounds when they breathe. Seeking veterinary assistance is vital to diagnose the cause and provide appropriate treatment to prevent further complications.

Digestive Issues

Ducks exhibiting persistent diarrhea, changes in appetite, constipation, foul smelling, or bloody droppings is a clear sign to seek veterinary assistance. Immediately consult the veterinarian and share the signs and symptoms you have noted for effective diagnosis and treatment.

Egg Laying Issues

When your duck stays too long in the nesting area, does not lay eggs regularly, and produces abnormal eggs, that indicates issues with the reproductive system. Taking it for a checkup by a certified veterinarian is the next step here.

Lameness or Mobility Issues

Injuries and certain medical conditions can cause ducks to experience issues with standing and walking and problems affecting their feet and legs. A professional veterinary evaluation is essential to accurately diagnose the problem and recommend appropriate treatments to improve their mobility and quality of life.

Injuries

Ducks can sustain injuries from various sources, and wounds, cuts, fractures, or conditions like bumblefoot (foot infections) can compromise their health. Seeking veterinary care for prompt and proper treatment is crucial to prevent infections, manage pain, and ensure optimal healing.

Parasite Infestations

Both internal and external parasites can adversely affect ducks' health. Suppose you observe signs of infestation, such as visible parasites on their skin or feathers, weight loss, weakness, or poor growth. In that case, it's essential to involve a veterinarian. Timely intervention can prevent parasites from causing further harm and discomfort to your ducks.

Sudden Deaths

Unexpected deaths within your flock should raise concern. While some deaths might occur naturally, sudden losses may indicate the presence of contagious diseases that could spread. Consulting a veterinarian can help you determine the cause and appropriate steps to prevent further losses.

Visible Symptoms

Any physical changes in ducks' appearance, such as swelling, discoloration, open sores, or abnormal growths, require professional evaluation. A veterinarian can accurately diagnose the condition, recommend treatments, and prevent potential complications.

Decreased Egg Production

A sudden drop in egg production or changes in egg quality, such as thin shells or unusual shapes, may signal reproductive issues. Seeking veterinary advice can help diagnose and address these problems to ensure the health of your ducks and their egg-laying capabilities.

Eye or Nasal Issues

Ducks with symptoms like eye discharge, swelling, redness, or nasal discharge may be experiencing eye or respiratory infections. Consulting a veterinarian is necessary to prevent further discomfort and complications.

Unexplained Weight Loss

Significant weight loss in ducks could indicate various health problems, including infections, parasites, or internal issues. Veterinary assistance is crucial for identifying the underlying cause and determining the best action.

Neurological Signs

Ducks displaying neurological symptoms like head tilting, tremors, seizures, or abnormal behavior require immediate veterinary evaluation. A professional assessment is necessary to determine the cause and provide appropriate care.

Changes in Vocalizations

Ducks communicate through vocalizations. If you notice one becoming unusually quiet or displaying new vocal patterns, it could indicate distress or illness. A veterinarian can assess the situation and recommend appropriate actions.

Flock-Wide Health Issues

If multiple ducks in your flock exhibit similar symptoms or a sudden decline in the overall health of your ducks, it may suggest a contagious disease. Veterinary consultation is essential to prevent disease spread and ensure proper treatment for affected ducks. Closely observing your ducks for behavior, appearance, or symptom changes is critical to their well-being. If you notice any concerning signs, seeking professional help from a veterinarian experienced in avian care is crucial for early diagnosis, effective treatment, and the long-term health of your duck flock.

Routine Checkups

Handling routine check-ups for your ducks requires careful planning, attentive observation, and a strong partnership with a skilled avian veterinarian. Regular veterinary visits are essential to monitor your ducks' health, identify emerging concerns, and ensure their well-being.

Here's a comprehensive guide on managing routine check-ups for your ducks:

- Begin by researching and establishing a relationship with a qualified avian veterinarian.
- Look for someone experienced in treating ducks or poultry, ideally located conveniently for regular visits.
- Contact the avian veterinarian to schedule routine check-up appointments for your ducks.
- Follow their recommended schedule, which may vary based on age, health history, and specific needs.
- Before the visit, compile a detailed record of your ducks' health history, including vaccinations, treatments, and previous health issues.
- Create a list of questions or concerns you'd like to discuss during the check-up.
- Make sure your ducks are comfortable and secure in a well-ventilated carrier or crate for transportation.

Discussing Things with the Veterinarian

During the check-up, allow the veterinarian to conduct a thorough physical examination of each duck. This involves assessing their weight, body condition, eyes, beak, feet, wings, and overall health. Take advantage of this time to share any observations or changes in behavior you've noticed since the last visit. Seek advice on diet, housing, disease prevention, and general care. The veterinarian may recommend diagnostic tests such as fecal exams, blood tests, or swabs to screen for potential health issues if necessary. Adhere to their recommendations for vaccinations, deworming, and other preventive measures tailored to your ducks' needs and potential disease risks.

The veterinarian will discuss potential treatment options, medications, and care instructions if they find any health issues. Make sure you understand the recommended treatment plan, including details about dosage, administration, and follow-up instructions. Don't hesitate to ask questions about duck care, behavior, diet, housing, or any other concerns you may have. Their expertise is a valuable resource. After the check-up, closely follow their guidance.

Chapter 7: The Beauty of the Duck Egg

Duck eggs aren't easy to crack because they have thicker shells than chicken eggs. Still, they should be handled with care. Collecting, maintaining, and storing duck eggs isn't a simple task. It takes time and effort, but it is worth it to keep them fresh so you can take advantage of their many health benefits.

Collecting, maintaining, and storing duck eggs isn't a simple task.
https://pixabay.com/photos/egg-duck-green-nest-nature-spring-4067035/

This chapter covers everything related to duck eggs. It will discuss their unique qualities, explain how to handle and take care of them, and provide simple and delicious recipes based on them.

Collecting and Handling Duck Eggs

Ducks lay eggs at night, so when you wake up the next day, they will be ready for you to collect. Let them out of their cages to exercise and forage while you look for the eggs.

Collect what you find right away; if you don't, they will nest with their eggs and stop producing. If you are raising them for eggs, you can't afford to go for days without new ones. So, schedule an hour every morning to go on a scavenger hunt in your ducks' coop.

Count the eggs first. If the number is low, this indicates that one or more of the ducks haven't yet produced any. They will most likely lay the eggs while they are outside. Keep an eye on them to spot where they lay. Usually, they choose the same spot every time, so this will make it easier to find them in the future.

Look for the eggs in their nesting boxes, housing area, and bedding. Check every corner because ducks can sometimes hide their eggs to protect them. This can take time and effort, but you'll soon familiarize yourself with their habits and learn their preferred locations.

The process of collecting the eggs is simple. You don't need any special equipment or even gloves. Simply remove the eggs with your hands, then place them in a small basket.

Tips for Handling Duck Eggs

- Wash your hands before and after you handle the eggs to protect the baby duckling from bacteria.
- Be careful when placing the eggs in the basket. Put them slowly and gently so they won't crack or break.
- Make sure the basket is made of solid materials so it won't break and damage the eggs.

Maintaining Egg Hygiene

While collecting the eggs is easy, the tricky part is cleaning them. Duck eggs are harder to clean than chicken eggs. They are usually covered with a gray layer that resembles a film and has an unpleasant odor.

Follow these steps to make the process easier for you.

Instructions:

1. After collecting the eggs, take the basket back home.
2. Using a clean, damp piece of cloth, wipe off the manure and mud.
3. Clean off the gray film with a kitchen scrubber.
4. Next, remove the bloom from the eggs by rinsing them in warm water, then clean them with a paper towel.

Some people prefer to leave the bloom because they believe it makes the eggs fresh for long periods and protects them from bacteria and air. Others claim that if you are going to sell your eggs or use them right away, you shouldn't worry about the shelf life. Consider the two opinions and choose what is best for you.

Eggs covered with blooms look unappetizing, so if shelf life isn't a concern, remove it. However, if you aren't going to sell the eggs and the bloom doesn't bother you, keep it. If you want to wash it, use warm water. Never wash the eggs with cold water, and avoid soaking them because they will get contaminated.

Storing Duck Eggs

After collecting and cleaning the eggs, you should properly store them to prevent spoilage, prolong their shelf life, and guarantee they will remain fresh for a long time.

Instructions:

1. Place them in an egg carton or container with the pointy end down to protect them from bacteria.
2. Label it with the date.
3. Store the carton in a cool place, preferably a refrigerator.
4. Place the eggs in the refrigerator to stabilize their temperature. If you store them on the door, their temperature will change every time you open it.
5. Use them for cooking, frying, or baking, just like chicken eggs.

Duck eggs will only last for three weeks at room temperature. Storing them in a refrigerator will give them a four-month shelf life. However, if you wash the eggs, they will only last for about five or six weeks in the fridge.

Duck eggs can easily go bad, but there is a simple test you can do to check if they are still fresh or not.

Instructions:

1. Fill a large glass jar or the kitchen sink with water.
2. Place one egg at a time in the water.
3. Fresh eggs will lay on their side or sink to the bottom.
4. Eggs that are starting to lose their freshness will sink but stand on one end. They are still safe but use them right away, preferably in baking.
5. Bad eggs will float. These aren't safe to use, so throw them away.

The Unique Qualities of Duck Eggs

There is a reason duck eggs are so popular, and more and more people prefer them over chicken eggs. They have unique qualities that set them apart, and they go beyond the delicious taste and nutritional benefits.

Long Shelf Life

Duck eggs have a longer shelf life than chicken eggs because they are larger, harder to crack, and have thicker membranes and shells. So they will remain fresh and delicious for long periods.

Creamier Taste

They contain high levels of proteins, vitamins, minerals, healthy fats, and more yolk than egg whites ratio. This gives them a much smoother, creamier, and richer taste than chicken eggs.

Large Size

They are noticeably larger than chicken eggs. It is then more economical to raise ducks for their eggs than chicken.

Great for Baking

Thanks to their high levels of proteins and fats, duck eggs are great for baking. They produce light cookies and bread that will melt in your mouth, high soufflés and meringues, and fluffier and more delicious cakes. They have the same culinary uses as chicken eggs, except they are tastier and creamier.

However, they can have a rubbery texture if you overcook them due to their low water content.

Contain More Nutrients

Ducks that are allowed to forage will produce eggs rich in nutrients. One egg can contain higher levels of iron, folate, choline, fatty acids,

Omega-3, and Vitamins A and D than chicken eggs.

Different Types of Protein

Duck eggs contain a different type of protein than their counterpart. You can safely consume duck eggs if you are allergic to chicken eggs.

A More Eggy Taste

Duck eggs have a more eggy taste than any other bird. Although an egg's flavor mainly depends on the bird's diet, a duck's egg has a unique taste. Foraging feed plays a huge role here as well. Ducks that can eat whatever they want from nature produce eggs with a unique flavor.

More Expensive

If you plan to sell the eggs, you'll be happy to know that duck eggs are more expensive than chicken eggs. Since they are harder to find, have better and unique qualities, and are great for baking, many chefs and high-end restaurants favor them. You won't have any trouble selling them.

Now that you have learned about the many unique qualities of duck eggs, let's discover some simple and fun recipes to make creamy and delicious dishes!

Duck Egg Quiche with Seasonal Vegetables

This is a tasty dish you can eat for breakfast, brunch, lunch, or dinner. You can change the recipe and experiment with different types of vegetables.

Ingredients:
- 4 duck eggs
- 6 ounces of baby spinach
- 2 minced garlic cloves
- 1 homemade dough or pie crust
- 1 diced shallot
- 4 ounces of shredded cheddar cheese
- 1 cup of whole milk
- 1 teaspoon of sea salt
- 1 tablespoon of olive oil

Instructions:

1. Preheat your oven to 350°F.

2. Prepare the dough by rolling it out and placing it on a pie plate. If you are using store-bought pie crust, follow the instructions on the package.

3. Next, pour the olive oil into a large pan, place it on a stove, and heat it over medium-high heat.

4. Wait until it is hot, then add the shallots. Let them sauté for three minutes.

5. Then add the spinach and garlic and leave it to cook until the spinach wilts.

6. Pour the mixture into the base of the pie dough to form a layer.

7. Crack the duck eggs into a small bowl, then mix until the yolk breaks.

8. Add the salt, half the cheddar cheese, and milk to the eggs, then whisk to mix them together.

9. Pour the mixture over the spinach mixture, then spread the rest of the cheese.

10. Put the mixture in the oven and leave it to bake for fifty minutes.

11. Get it out of the oven and leave it to cool down for five minutes. Then slice and serve while it is still warm.

Classic Duck Egg Pasta Carbonara

This is a popular Italian dish that you can make for lunch.

Ingredients:

- 1 large, chopped bundle of parsley
- 1 large minced garlic clove
- 3 whisked duck egg yolks
- 200 grams of dried Linguine (a type of Italian pasta)
- 40 grams of grated Parmesan cheese
- 50 grams of diced smoked pancetta (type of pork)
- 100 grams of cubed smoked pancetta
- Pinch of pepper to taste
- Grated Parmesan (for serving)

Instructions:

1. Pour water into a large pot and add salt, then leave it to boil.

2. Put the dried linguine in the pot and leave it to cook for eleven minutes.

3. Prepare the sauce while the pasta is cooking.

4. Place a large empty frying pan over the stove and leave it over low heat.

5. Next, add the diced pancetta, then gradually increase the heat over a few minutes until the fats melt away from the pancetta and it turns crisp.

6. Remove the pancetta, but leave the fat in the pan.

7. Lower the heat to medium-high, add the cubed pancetta to the pan, and leave it to cook with the fat for three minutes.

8. Next, add the garlic to the pan and leave them to cook until the pancetta starts to crisp.

9. Remove the pan from the stove.

10. Take the linguine out of the pot and drain it. Don't discard the water.

11. Add the linguine to the pan, then splash some of the pasta water over it.

12. Spread the grated parmesan and the duck egg yolk over the pan.

13. Mix the yolk with the pancetta and linguine and leave them to gently cook.

14. Add more cooking pasta water to make the sauce glossy and loose.

15. Season with the parsley and black pepper.

16. Twist the pasta onto plates with a long fork, then sprinkle the crisp pancetta.

17. Sprinkle more grated parmesan, then serve while it's hot.

Duck Egg French Toast with Caramelized Apples

Enjoy this sweet treat for breakfast or brunch. Serve it hot.

Ingredients for Caramelized Apples:

- ½ teaspoon of cinnamon
- ½ cup of sugar
- ½ cup of water
- ¼ cup of butter
- 2 apples

Ingredients for French Toast:

- 2 duck eggs
- 4 slices of bread
- 2 tablespoons of frying butter
- 2 tablespoons of almond milk
- ½ teaspoon of cinnamon
- 2 tablespoons of granulated sugar

Instructions:

1. Peel the apples, then cut them into slices or cubes.
2. Put the apples in a pot, then add half a cup of sugar, water, and butter.
3. Leave it to cook over the stove for fifteen minutes and stir frequently to prevent it from sticking or burning.
4. Once the apples soften, remove them from the stove.
5. Break the duck eggs in a small bowl, then beat them together with a whisk.
6. Add the cinnamon, almond milk, and two tablespoons of sugar to the duck eggs, then whisk to mix together.
7. Dip each slice of the bread from both sides in the egg mix.
8. Heat a skillet over medium-high, then add the butter and let it melt.
9. Add the French toast and let it cook from both sides until it turns gold.

10. Put the caramelized apples over the French toast and serve hot.

Garlic and Chili Duck Egg Fried Rice

This Chinese dish is easy to make. You don't have to use the same ingredients in the recipe. You can experiment with different ones and get creative.

Ingredients:
- 2 lightly beaten duck eggs
- 3 tablespoons of peanut oil or duck fat
- 3 chopped cloves of garlic
- 2 tablespoons of soy sauce
- 2 peeled and diced carrots
- 3 chopped scallions (separate the green and white parts)
- 3 cups of cooled and cooked rice
- 1 to 3 chopped hot and small chilies
- 1 cup of fresh peas
- ½ pound of shredded duck meat, preferably leftover
- 1 tablespoon of sesame oil

Instructions:
1. Heat a large frying pan over the stove.
2. Next, add the peanut oil or duck fat and leave it to cook until it smokes.
3. Add the white part of the scallions, chilies, and garlic to the frying pan. Stir for thirty seconds.
4. Add the peas, carrots, rice, and duck meat, then stir for two minutes.
5. Push the ingredients to the side of the frying pan, then add the duck eggs.
6. Let it set while swirling with a chopstick.
7. Stir fry it into the rice and leave it for one minute. Don't touch it.
8. It should turn brown and crispy.
9. Next, pour the soy sauce over the rice edges, then mix.
10. Take it off the heat, then add the sesame oil.

Decadent Duck Egg Chocolate Mousse

This delicious chocolate mousse is creamy and tasty and can be the perfect dessert for you and your loved ones.

Ingredients:

- 3 large duck eggs
- 1 cup of cold and heavy cream
- 2 tablespoons of strong coffee
- 4 ½ ounces of chopped bittersweet chocolate
- 1 tablespoon of sugar
- 2 tablespoons of cubed and unsalted butter
- Whipped cream (optional)
- Raspberries (optional)

Instructions:

1. Whip the heavy cream until it softens, then let it chill.
2. Place the heavy coffee, butter, and chocolate in a double boiler over steamy, hot water. Stir until it turns smooth.
3. Remove the double boiler from the stove and leave it to cool or until the chocolate feels warm.
4. After the mixture cools, whip the egg whites until they turn creamy and form a shape.
5. Add the sugar, then whip again until the egg whites form stiff peaks.
6. Add the egg yolks, then stir.
7. Add ⅓ of the whipped cream to the chocolate mix and stir until it loosens.
8. Then add half the egg whites and stir.
9. Add the rest of the egg white, and sir.
10. Add the whipped cream, then stir.
11. Serve the mousse with a spoon in small dishes.
12. Add the whipped cream and raspberries on top for decoration, then leave them in the refrigerator for eight to twenty-four hours.

Smoked Salmon Eggs Benedict

If you love seafood, you'll enjoy this dish. This recipe is similar to eggs benedict with a couple of twists.

Eggs and Hollandaise Sauce Ingredients:

- 3 tablespoons of unsalted butter
- 1 sprig of fresh basil
- ¼ teaspoon of cardamom
- 1 sprig of fresh tarragon
- 2 coriander seeds
- 1 bay leaf
- 2 white peppercorns
- 1 minced shallot
- 1 minced garlic clove
- 4 duck egg yolks
- ⅓ cup of water

Smoked Salmon Topper Ingredients:

- Pinch of cayenne pepper
- 1 tablespoon of freshly squeezed lemon juice
- 1 tablespoon of mayonnaise
- ½ teaspoon of Dijon mustard
- 4-6 slices of smoked salmon
- 2 duck eggs
- White wine vinegar

Instructions:

1. Place the basil, cardamom, tarragon, coriander, bay leaf, peppercorns, shallot, and garlic in a small saucepan.
2. Leave it to boil on slow heat.
3. Reduce the heat to low, then let it simmer for ten minutes.
4. Strain with a sieve or cheesecloth, then set the liquid aside and discard the remaining ingredients.
5. Place the egg yolks in a double boiler.
6. Whisk until the yolks turn soft and fluffy.

7. Add the butter to the mixture while whisking.

8. Keep whisking until it thickens.

9. Remove the sauce from the stove, cover it with foil, and place it in a warm spot.

10. Put the duck eggs in boiling water and sprinkle some salt over it, then pour a splash of white wine vinegar.

11. Once they are cooked, remove the eggs from the water with a spoon.

12. Put the small salmon mixture over the poached duck eggs.

13. Pour the sauce over the dish.

Creamy Duck Egg Flan

This is a delicious dessert you can prepare and store in the fridge for two days and serve to your guests on a warm summer day.

Ingredients:

- 2 duck yolks
- 4 duck eggs
- 1 tablespoon of vanilla extract
- 1 can of condensed milk
- 1 ¼ cups of granulated sugar
- Pinch of salt

Instructions:

1. Preheat the oven to 350°F.

2. Place the vanilla extract, salt, condensed milk, and whipping cream in a saucepan.

3. Bring it to low or medium heat and stir frequently.

4. Remove the saucepan from the stove and let the mixture steep for fifteen minutes.

5. Next, get another saucepan and mix one cup of sugar with ⅓ of water.

6. Leave it on medium heat and stir until the sugar dissolves.

7. Reduce to low heat and let it simmer until the mixture thickens and caramelizes.

8. Pour the sugar mixture into custard cups.

9. Put on oven mitts and swirl the sides of the mixture in each cup.

10. Place the cups in a large baking pan.

11. Blend the egg yolks and whole eggs with the milk mixture.

12. Pour the mixture into the cups (divide them evenly).

13. Boil water and pour it into the baking pan.

14. Put it in the oven and let it bake for forty minutes.

15. Next, remove the pan from the oven and leave the cups to cool down.

Ducks lay eggs every day. Check your flock in the morning and collect them right away. Handle the eggs with care to avoid cracking them. Clean them from the mud using a damp or dry towel. Avoid washing them, or you'll shorten their shelf life. If you use them right away, you can wash them to remove the bloom since it is unsanitary.

Duck eggs are unique in more ways than one. They are large, delicious, creamy, and have a long shelf life. You can incorporate them in many recipes, and they can alter the flavor and texture of your dish. They also have many health benefits, and you can use them instead of chicken eggs in any recipe.

Chapter 8: Ethical Considerations and Best Practices

Raising ducks may not be as hip or profitable as chicken farming, but the practice is gradually on the rise. It has even become an emerging trend in many parts of the world.

Ducks, especially ducklings, are absolutely adorable. You can train them to a certain extent or simply play with them outdoors. Imprinted ducklings will stay with you throughout their lifespan. Duck eggs are larger and more nutritious than chicken eggs. Last but not least, these waterfowl are a great source of meat, too.

Ducks, especially ducklings, are absolutely adorable.
https://pixabay.com/photos/ducklings-pair-birds-beaks-animals-1853178/

If you have a passion for poultry farming, there is no reason why you should not raise ducks. Don't just jump on the bandwagon to gain acceptance or popularity by posting cute duckling pictures and videos on social media. There's nothing wrong with that, but it shouldn't be your only reason for raising these adorable animals.

Raise ducks for the right reasons, and more importantly, raise them the right way. To do that, you'll need to understand the moral ambiguities surrounding various techniques.

Ethical Considerations of Raising Ducks

Raising ducks as pets doesn't have any ethical conflicts, except one, and it's a big one. It's the universal argument against keeping all animals as pets. Here's how the logic goes. In a democracy, you choose to be under the president's authority. You have chosen that person to govern your country. They have your consent, and you have their consent to govern you.

Take an example closer to home. An employee works under their employer. They have chosen to work under the employer's authority. The employer has consented to let the employee work under them. There is mutual consent here.

In the case of animals or birds, you are the only one who consents to place them under your authority and make them your pet since the creature cannot communicate its consent. It may learn to love you over time, but while adopting or purchasing the being, it may hate you for taking away its freedom. You may like how it looks and behaves, but it doesn't know its feelings for you yet.

In the case of animals or birds, you are the only one who consents to place them under your authority and make them your pet since the creature cannot communicate its consent.

The situation is akin to a stalker kidnapping their prey. The kidnapped person may hate the stalker for taking their freedom. Over time, if they are treated well, they may begin to like their abductor. It's the harsh truth of keeping pets. You know that the animal or bird is better off with you, but it doesn't know that. It's the way of life, the survival of the fittest. Chalk it up to the greater good and move on.

Alternatively, are you planning to raise ducks only for practical purposes, like the production of eggs and meat? Your apprehension about becoming too attached to them is perfectly understandable. It doesn't mean that you should entirely ignore caring for them. Did you know that healthy, well-cared ducks give better eggs and meat? Either way, there are a few ethical considerations (don'ts) you need to consider.

• Don't Keep a Duck without Company

Dogs and cats may thrive with your company alone. Ducks, however, can rarely survive without fellow ducks or ducklings. Even if they do, they will remain troubled throughout their lifespan and die a miserable death. Just like humans, they feel loneliness and sorrow. They need to socialize, procreate, and communicate.

• Don't Keep a Duck in Your House

Just like most other birds, ducks value their freedom. They may not fly much, but they love swimming and roaming around under the open sky. If you keep your ducks in the house, they will eventually become overwhelmed with negative emotions, and they may lash out by making a lot of noise or even getting violent.

• Don't Let Them Roam Free All the Time

Ducks require proper care, and ducklings are even more so. They have a lot, from the bold crows to the ferocious bobcats. If you let them roam free in your neighborhood, a hawk may swoop in and carry away the ducks, or a raccoon may steal the ducklings. Be sure to build a secure coop for them to play in or keep your backyard door shut.

• Don't Keep Ducks Away from Water

Ducks are called waterfowl for good reason. They bathe and play in water. They require water to clean their feathers and to clear their eyes and nostrils free of dirt. Additionally, they love to splash around in a pool, swim for long hours, and submerge their heads to clean their entire body.

• Choose the Breed According to Your Requirements

Different breeds of ducks specialize in different actions. For instance, Khaki Campbell ducks produce the maximum number of eggs among all other breeds. On the other hand, the White Pekin is best known for its meat quality. If you want a pet duck, you may consider a Magpie. It's easy on the eye and rarely has any problems - a perfect beginner's duck.

• Don't Raise Ducks Just to Try Out Poultry Farming

Ducks aren't ideal for beginning your poultry farming venture. Try chickens or dogs if you are new to animal and bird care. Ducks are primarily for experienced caretakers. The big reason is their lifespan. Ducks can live for nearly 20 years.

Down the road, if you don't wish to care for them anymore, you can't just leave them in the wild and hope they survive. They probably won't survive a week in the wild.

While abandoning any animals or birds under your care is cruel, duck desertion is especially heartless. Admittedly, they can survive in a flock, as you may have read in a previous chapter. Domesticated ducks have an entirely different disposition. They may be less careful and more prone to being attacked by predators.

Now that you know what you should not do while raising ducks, here's what you can do while adhering to the ethics of the entire process.

Best Practices of Raising Ducks

So far, you learned the basic and advanced techniques of raising ducks. It's time to take a look at everything you can do to get the best out of this. The best practices vary depending on your reasons for raising ducks.

Raising Ducklings

Ducks need a lot of care, and ducklings need even more. Since they are lovable little creatures, you won't feel the burden of your chores one bit.

- **Feeding:** Ducklings need to be given food different from ducks only for the first two or three weeks of their life. You must ensure that their feed is high in protein (at least 20%). You also need to give them a decent amount (around 0.45 mg per 500 grams body weight) of niacin (vitamin B-3) per day. Niacin deficiency may cause serious problems, ranging from lameness to body deformities.

- **Watering:** Did you know that your duckling's health will begin to deteriorate within just a few hours without water? They require water after waking up, before and after eating, before playing, while playing, after playing, and before going to sleep. You get the gist!

On average, a baby duck will consume half a gallon of water each week, which doesn't seem much. That's because they also tend to splash around in the water, spilling most of it out. It is ideal to have a water fountain to pump clean water from time to time. But if you are using a tub or a bucket, make sure to refill it with clean water every few hours.

- **Swimming:** Typically, ducklings can learn to swim soon after hatching. The problem lies in their ability to fend off the cold. Adult ducks don't catch the chill after swimming because they secrete a layer of waterproofing oil on their feathers. Ducklings need around four to five weeks to start producing that oil and protect themselves from the cold.

You can place your ducklings in the water earlier than four weeks, but ensure they don't stay in too long. As soon as they are out of the water, keep a heat lamp over them or place them in a brooder so they won't become cold.

- **Brooding**: Ducklings can be brooded in any type of brooding house, but it's best done in a nest. You may use a heat lamp or a warming plate. Keep it well-ventilated with a constant supply of water. They only need enough space to move around a bit, so don't make the nest too big. Set the temperature to about 85 degrees F, and you may reduce it by around 5-6 degrees each week. They only need to brood for the first two to four weeks after hatching.

- **Bedding**: Ducklings are most comfortable in a bed made of straw, which is also moisture-absorbent. Since ducklings make a lot of mess, you'll need to change the bedding often, and straw is easy to find and replace. The shorter the stems, the more at ease the ducklings will be. Other bedding alternatives include old hay, pine shavings, or mulch.

Raising Ducks for Meat

Ducks are usually ready to be butchered for meat after 7-8 weeks, which is why they cannot be raised like pet ducks.

- **Breeds/Species:** Not all breeds of ducks are ideal for meat. A few breeds aren't to everyone's taste, like the shoveler duck. On the other hand, a few others are perfect for human consumption. If you are thinking of raising an assortment of meat ducks, consider starting with a Pekin or a Muscovy. You can later progress to a Moulard or a Rouen.

- **Feeding:** Since you'll be using the ducks for meat as soon as they are ready, you'll need to feed them a diet very high in protein. The recommended proportion is 25% in the early stages while gradually bringing it down to around 20% in the 7th or 8th week.

- **Watering**: Keep a constant source of drinking water in the vicinity, like a duck fountain. Make sure that it's clean at all times because you'll be consuming what they are drinking. Mature ducks will need more water than ducklings (roughly 0.20 to 0.50 gallons).

- **Swimming**: Ducks don't need to swim, but they will be happier if they can at least once a day. Put up a shallow fountain or bowl for ducklings so that they don't drown. Once they mature and can float around for hours, let them play in a deeper and wider pool.

- **Brooding:** Since your eight-week-old ducks won't be producing eggs, their brooding house should be constructed like that of ducklings. Maintain a temperature of around 80F.

- **Bedding:** You don't need to switch your duckling's bedding when they mature into a duck. If you have been using straw so far, then stick with straw. They have gotten used to it underneath them while sleeping. If you change the material to hay in the middle of their growth, they may start feeling uncomfortable.

Raising Ducks for Eggs

If you are raising ducks only for consuming or selling eggs, then it's not a feasible option. The costs of nurturing ducks will be much higher than the eggs purchased at a supermarket. You may also want to consider raising them for meat or just keeping them as pets.

Hens generally start laying eggs when they are six to seven months old. They may keep producing a relatively high quantity of eggs until around eight years of age, after which their egg-laying capacity gradually begins to decline, completely stopping around two years later. If you are raising them for meat as well, it is recommended that you slaughter them when they are 18 months old.

- **Breeds/Species:** While all female ducks lay eggs, the number of eggs laid per year varies from species to species. The Khaki Campbell is preferred by most duck egg lovers in the world. It lays around 300 eggs per year and is also one of the easiest breeds to take care of. Runner ducks, primarily from Malaysia, also can reach the 300 mark. For a decent range of around 200-250 eggs per year, you may consider raising Magpie, Saxony, Pekin, Ancona, or Welsh Harlequin.

- **Feeding:** When they are in the duckling stage, they will need around 20% protein and a decent amount of niacin. Their (both ducklings and ducks) feed should be especially rich in calcium (around 4%) to ensure strong eggs. Most duck feeds available in the market contain the right proportion of nutrients, but it doesn't hurt to check before buying.

- **Watering**: As with ducklings and meat ducks, egg layers also need a lot of water to produce good-quality eggs. Keep a flowing fountain near their home, often refreshed with clean water. A pond will require you to clean the water soon after they drink it.

- **Swimming**: Egg layers swim the same amount of time as meat ducks, so be sure to construct an outdoor pool.

- **Brooding:** Different breeds of ducks brood for different time periods. The Khaki Campbell requires at least three weeks of brooding, whereas the Pekin may be done within two weeks. The brooding house should be the same as that mentioned for ducklings. Remember, moisture, ventilation, and heat are key to ensure successful brooding of ducks.

- **Bedding:** Ducks need ventilation as much as they require protection from predators. Their coop needs to have many windows and a roof to keep flying carnivores at bay. You don't need to create special bedding for adult ducks. They will forage the necessary materials and build a nest on their own. To help them out, you may just place a pile of straw or a bale of old hay nearby.

Raising Ducks as Pets or Ornaments

Do you wish to show off your ducks to your friends and neighbors or on social media? Try raising breeds that are known for their beauty. Ornamental ducks aren't usually known for the taste of their meat, and their eggs are simply an added bonus (they may produce around 100-200 eggs per year). With pet ducks, your primary focus should be on their health.

With pet ducks, your main focus should be on their health.

- **Breeds/Species**: You need to be very careful while choosing the breed of your pets. All ducklings look adorable, but the question is how they appear as grownups. Do you want to add a splash of color to your coop? Go for the Mallard, Cayuga, and Wood duck breeds. Do you wish to create a sober atmosphere? You can never go wrong with Rouen or Buff Orpington ducks.

- **Feeding:** Feeding your ducklings is the same as mentioned in a previous section. Once it grows into an adult, you can let it forage for food on its own. They will eat insects, bugs, earthworms, and even certain plant leaves and roots. For proper nutrition and safety from predators, always keep their feed bowl filled so they won't have to venture out into the wild.

- **Watering:** The water requirements of pet and ornamental ducks are the same as all other breeds (0.25 to 0.50 gallons per day).

- **Swimming**: They need to swim often – like all other duck breeds – so build a sufficiently large pool within reach.

- **Brooding:** Egg layers, even if they lay fewer eggs than other species, need to brood for a set number of weeks. Their brooding coop need be no different than that of other breeds.

- **Bedding**: Straw is the most commonly used bedding for pet ducks, just like their meat and egg-laying counterparts.

Home Duck Slaughtering Tips

As you know by now, most meat ducks are ready to be butchered after about 7 weeks. Nevertheless, it is prudent to wait for a few months before slaughtering them so that you can get more meat out of them. Wait times differ for different species. For instance, Muscovy ducks grow to the ideal weight of six pounds in about four months, whereas you can get a 10-pound Pekin within just two months. Once they are ready, heed the following tips to get optimum meat from your ducks.

- Don't feed the ducks for around 14 hours before butchering to make the process easier.
- Killing a duck with a killing cone is easier and more humane, but if you can't find a large enough cone, you may consider hanging it with a rope tied to its legs and then killing it.
- The actual process of butchering starts with either skinning or plucking. Make sure that the butcher knife is sharp while skinning. Before plucking, you need to scald the duck in a pot of heated water. Then, simply pluck it by hand.
- Set your butchering station under a tap or near a lake to ensure a quick, easy clean.
- Place the butchered meat in the fridge for 24 hours before transferring it to the freezer.

Humane Duck Killing

- Place the duck upside down in the killing cone. This inverted posture will make its final moments more peaceful and relaxing.
- Grab its head by the beak and slice your knife slightly above its jawline. That's where its main artery is located. It won't feel the pain at all as it quickly bleeds out.

Chapter 9: Integration, Companionship, and Breeding

Much like humans have complex societal structures and norms, ducks have their ways of establishing order. To raise ducks, it is necessary to understand their social order so that you can meet them on their level. Recognizing that different environments will impact your birds in varying ways is the beginning of understanding duck behavior. You have to meet in the middle by interpreting their body language and behavioral responses. Observing your ducks can reveal details about their desires and needs.

Attention to detail is key for compassionately raising these interesting birds. Much like humans, they can be cryptic and difficult to understand if you are uninformed. Just like you must observe tone and body language to fully grasp what a person is communicating, for ducks, you can interpret their mood, mindset, and personality by the specifics of how they engage with you and your other animals. Through this subtle communication, you'll find out how unique each duck is based on their temperaments and interactions with you. The duck kingdom is full of characters, so we are in for a turbulent but fun journey. Do not let the little humps throw you off course. When it comes to these animals, perseverance is key.

Ducks wear their hearts on their wings. If you know what to look for, you'll immediately know when they are unhappy. Ducks demonstrate complex interpersonal interactions, from their bonds with caregivers to their socialization within groups. Understanding these behaviors can help you breed ducks and create a home that maximizes their well-being. Respect and patience are the pillars that hold up successful duck rearing. Making decisions with the best interests of your ducks in mind will result in a happy and healthy flock.

Depending on your desired outcomes, you must make a duck habitat that supports the goals you envision for your flock. Caring for ducks is approached differently if you are raising ducks for produce or keeping them as pets. Ducks can be aggressive, and they often bite people. To prevent injury to your birds or people they encounter, you must be aware of the warning signs of aggression and what is most conducive to a calm environment. In essence, if you play nice, your ducks will play nice. You just need to understand that they perceive the world differently from you, so communication requires a shift in perspective.

Meeting at the point of interspecies understanding is where the magic of duck-raising manifests. Once you learn to decode the sounds and actions of your ducks, you'll be given insight into their world. Furthermore, you'll open a doorway for your animals to connect with you. Ethical duck raising requires creating an environment that allows your ducks to be comfortable, calm, and content. As social creatures, ducks will form a relationship with you as a caregiver and with other members of your flock. You must facilitate desirable behavior because small mistakes can charge up aggressively intolerable ducks.

Social Interactions of Ducks

Ducks function within large social groups. It is possible to raise a solitary duck, but they will form bonds with you. Groups of ducks are called *paddlings*. Wild ducks migrate to follow favorable weather patterns, but domestic ducks typically stay in the area where they were raised. These dangerous migrations are part of the reason why ducks have formed such complex social structures. In nature, for ducks to survive, cooperation means the difference between paddling gracefully around a scenic pond or becoming a midday snack.

Ducks function within large social groups.
https://pixabay.com/photos/ducks-chicks-mallards-birds-7251870/

Ducks have evolved a linear social hierarchy known as a pecking order, especially when it comes to mating. The female ducks lay eggs according to who is the highest ranking. The lead gets to lay eggs first, with the other ducks following in descending order of importance. Male ducks, or drakes, also have a similar order, with the male lead getting to mate first. The hens guard their eggs as a collective. The pecking order also applies to feeding, with the lead ducks eating first and lower-ranking ducks eating last.

All breeds are not created equal. Some are docile, while others are more aggressive. You need to think about this before deciding which ducks you'll breed. Breeds like the Pekin duck guard their nests more aggressively, often resulting in conflict with people or other animals. When choosing a breed to raise, it is essential to weigh the dynamics of your property. If you have dogs, you may want to get a less aggressive breed because an altercation between a dog and a duck can have bloody consequences. Ducks will attack small children if they feel that their nests are being threatened, so if you have young ones running around, they need to be educated about how to behave around ducks. Preferably, you can choose a breed that is more well-suited for kids to interact with.

One way to reduce aggression is by separating the hens from the drakes. Both hens and drakes can be protective of their mating partners, which means keeping a mix of the two sexes doesn't often end well, especially among more aggressive breeds. Space can also become an issue because the evolutionary biology of ducks is catered to traveling long distances and moving around a lot. Therefore, keeping ducks inside your home is not advised because it can create distress for those who prefer spaciousness.

Bonding with Caregivers

The social inclinations of ducks make it easier to establish bonds with them. Unlike other bird species that are solitary and unable to care for you, ducks are sentimental beings. One of the key occurrences that highlight the social nature of ducks is the phenomenon of imprinting. When a duckling hatches in the wild, it will imprint on its mother and a few of its siblings. Imprinting is an attachment that is formed, which helps a duckling determine who it should follow. If you are the primary caregiver for a duckling, it will imprint on you, especially if no other ducks are around.

If a duck imprints on you, it will identify humans as part of its social circle for as long as it lives. This could help in an environment where ducks often interact with people. Wildlife specialists have warned against leading wild ducks to imprint on humans because it puts them at a disadvantage in the natural world. For domestic animals, imprinting is not an issue. Ducks that have imprinted on humans will not necessarily be socialized and friendly. The imprinting process means that ducks will not fear humans, which could have the adverse impact of leading to aggressive behavior.

Allowing your ducks to imprint on you is not advisable, even though it sounds like a great experience. Imprinted ducks are a far cry from the picturesque imagery of a princess dancing along a forest pathway with tame animals following as she sings high notes. Ducks that have imprinted on humans are at a disadvantage because they get stuck in a weird limbo of being unable to fully socialize with ducks or humans. Therefore, ducklings should spend most of their time with their mother to be fully socialized into the duck community. Caring for your ducklings is important at the early, vulnerable stage of their lives, but it cannot be done by sacrificing their long-term wellness.

Wild ducks that have imprinted on humans can never be released back into their natural habitats. Therefore, if your ducks have imprinted on you, it is a lifetime commitment. Domesticated ducks spend their entire lives on a farm or homestead, so human imprinting in that context is not as detrimental. Ducks are genetically wired to form strong relationships within their support system. Since you'll be raising ducks, you are now integrated into their social circle.

How to Introduce New Ducks to an Existing Flock

Since ducks can be confrontational, introducing new ones into your flock must be well-thought-out and planned. You cannot just dump a new duck in the pond and hope that everyone gets along. Just as humans have formalities and reservations about meeting new people, ducks must follow similar social protocols. First and foremost, before your new duck can get introduced to your flock, you must conduct a health evaluation. Ducks are resilient, but they can still fall ill. The medical evaluation of your new duck must include checks for respiratory illness, mobility issues, and parasites. Ducks are social and interact with one another in close proximity, so any infectious illness has the perfect mix of variables to spread quickly. During the period of medical evaluation, your new ducks should be quarantined.

The time you introduce new ducks is also important. The mating season of ducks is in the springtime. That is a terrible time to bring in new members. Hormones are going insane, so erratic behavior is almost guaranteed. Overzealous males can also hurt new females that are introduced into the flock.

Furthermore, females can also be competitive at this time due to their hormones, so this could lead to confrontations with a new hen. If you acquire new ducks during the mating season, it would be best to keep them separated until the season is over. The springtime can be volatile for ducks, so throwing someone new into the mix could be stirring the pot a little too much.

If you are tending multiple flocks, you can introduce the new duck to the group that you feel will be more welcoming. You could observe the interactions of your ducks daily so you can gauge which of your flocks are calmer. If a flock is already chaotic, it may be ill-advised to attempt to bring in any new ducks because that energy will get directed toward the newcomer. It will be easier if the flock that a new duck is introduced to is already docile and submissive. This submissive flock that you'll have the most ease with during introductions.

Any new ducks you wish to integrate must gradually be introduced to the flock. One method you can use is keeping the new duck separated but in an adjacent place where the ducks can interact without direct physical contact. This can give your flock time to adjust to the new member. Springing a sudden change can be jarring, so giving your ducks time to settle into the change is only fair. Remember that ducks form strong social bonds, so they have not yet connected with the new duck, who is an outsider. During this early integration period, you should closely monitor your ducks to make sure that nobody gets hurt.

Some fighting will occur at the initial stages of bringing a new duck into the flock. This conflict is normal because the group's social order must be established. The fighting is the ducks' way of organizing themselves into a neat hierarchy. Your observation will just be to ensure the fights do not get out of hand because you wouldn't want any of your ducks seriously injured. Feeding can be another issue when introducing new ducks. Observe how well your new ducks are eating because it is common for an original flock to shun new members from feeding areas. However, a new duck can be fully integrated into the flock after a couple of weeks with your help and guidance.

Mating Behaviors

The mating season is an interesting time for ducks. Just like human relationships, the love life of ducks can get complicated and competitive. Ducks communicate their mating intentions with body language. Their courting rituals include a lot of flirting. Males attract females with elaborate dance displays where they bob their heads and show off their feathers. An interested female will bob her head along with the male duck in an elaborate courting exercise.

Ducks' courting rituals include a lot of flirting.
https://pixabay.com/photos/rubber-ducks-wedding-wedding-couple-2402752/

Males will spread their wings and lift up their tails to show off their colorful secondary feathers to attract a female. The male will then submerge itself in water and pop back up, letting out a grunting whistle. This display is often done in groups so that a female can get her pick of the best suitor. Ducks use a variety of vocalizations and body language to communicate their intentions and feelings. Hissing is a sign of aggression, while other variations of quacks and honks communicate that they are happy or upset. These vocalizations can be used to collaborate, like when ducks fly together in formation.

Females who are interested in courtship will hold their heads low close to the water while swimming short distances. They will also bop their heads up and down to show their desire. Competition can become fierce since every female and male is trying to get the best conduit for their genetics. In the mating season, ducks will fight more and will be extra aggressive. Be aware that ducks may hurt you and your other animals in the mating season if you are not careful. Pay attention to their body language and vocalizations because they often provide warnings before they attack. A good habit to adopt during mating season is checking your ducks for injuries because of the increased risk of fighting during this period.

Ducks are semi-monogamous. Unlike some other bird species, like penguins that mate for life, ducks choose a new mate every season. The evolutionary advantage of this is the ability to choose the most suitable mates each year because they may have deteriorated over time. If you aim to breed your ducks, you must maintain an equal hen-to-drake ratio. This will minimize conflict and help you maintain a constant flow of new ducks by maximizing your breeding capabilities.

Nesting and Incubation

Ducks construct minimalistic nests on the ground made from twigs, reeds, and grass. If you want to harvest eggs, you should create a space with the appropriate requirements that a hen can use to construct a nest. Duck nests on the ground explain why they become protective after laying eggs. A nest on the ground is easily accessible to predators and can be trampled by mistake. To find nests, you should check reedy areas that are close to the water. Ducks are emotional and intelligent, so you should be careful and respectful when handling their nests or eggs. Approach the process of harvesting eggs with the utmost care.

As a breeder, you may want to ensure that all your eggs hatch. Therefore, you could incubate the eggs. Duck eggs take about 28 days to hatch inside an incubator. The humidity and temperature are important at this phase because slight changes can throw off this sensitive biological process. The humidity in the incubator should be set at 44% to 55% for the first 25 days. In the last three days, you can increase the humidity up to 65%. Your eggs should be turned at 180 degrees five times a day. You must be careful not to disturb the eggs too much. There is a pinpoint balance that must be reached with duck incubation. Some more sophisticated incubators turn the eggs automatically.

Raising Ducklings

Like any other young animal, ducklings require additional care. Your ducklings will be predominantly raised by their mother, or you'll hand-raise them in a brooder. If you are raising your ducklings without a hen, you are responsible for providing what the hen would have given the ducks, including food, warmth, shelter, and safety. The brooder in which your ducks are being raised must be soft and comfortable.

Temperature control is essential for raising healthy ducklings. The environment they live in should be 90 degrees. After a few days, you'll drop the temperature down to 85 degrees. You can then decrease the temperature by five degrees every week after that until they reach about thirty days old. It takes about three months for a duckling to grow fully. Heating is done with a lamp. If you see that your ducklings are huddling close together underneath the lamp, it means that they are getting cold. If your ducklings are panting and avoiding the lamp, they are getting too hot.

Ducklings swim from day one. You can start them off in a small container or even a bathtub before introducing them to a bigger body of water. They spend a large section of their time in the water. Ensuring your ducklings are happily swimming along is an exercise they will truly appreciate. The bigger your ducklings get, the more time they can spend outside in the sun and fresh air. Predators like cats, snakes, and birds are dangerous to your ducklings. As a mother will protect her brood, you must also keep a sharp eye out when the ducklings are in the yard. The bright yellow color of the feathers will slowly begin changing as they grow and is an indicator of maturity. They also have a specialized feed that you can get from qualified dealers, but they can also eat mealworms, chopped-up melon, and cooked oatmeal. Finally, ensure that your ducklings have a constant supply of drinking water in a small container.

Chapter 10: Challenges, Solutions and FAQs

Raising ducks becomes a breeze when you know the challenges that come with them. Maintaining the right approach and implementing adequate solutions will make your duck-raising journey enjoyable and hassle-free. Here's a quick refresher on the most common health issues and challenges.

Raising ducks might come with its set of challenges, but it is worth it.

https://www.pexels.com/photo/duckling-on-black-soil-during-daytime-162140/

Challenges in Duck Raising

Health Issues

Water Quality: Ducks are highly dependent on water. Make sure to provide them with clean, fresh water at all times. Stagnant or dirty water can lead to health problems, so change it regularly. Additionally, ducks should have access to a shallow pool to swim and clean themselves.

Parasites: Regularly inspect your ducks for external parasites like mites and lice. These can cause discomfort and various health issues. Consult a veterinarian to determine suitable treatments and preventive measures to keep your ducks parasite-free.

Respiratory Issues: Ducks develop respiratory illnesses, especially in humid and unsanitary living environments. Maintaining adequate ventilation and cleanliness can significantly prevent the growth of harmful bacteria or toxic gases like ammonia.

Botulism: Ducks are susceptible to botulism, a potentially fatal illness caused by toxins produced by bacteria in contaminated water. Keep their living area clean and remove any potential sources of contamination. Do not feed them spoiled or moldy food.

Aggressive Behavior

Socialization: Ducks have a pecking order and can exhibit aggression, especially when introducing new members to the flock. Gradually introduce new ducks, allowing them time to establish their hierarchy. Monitor their interactions and provide hiding spots to reduce stress.

Space: Overcrowding can lead to aggression. Make sure your ducks have enough space in their living area to move around comfortably. A lack of space can also contribute to stress and health problems.

Hiding Spots: Ducks need places to hide or escape. Provide hiding spots like boxes or bushes in their enclosure to allow them to retreat if they need to.

Dietary Concerns

Balanced Diet: Ducks require a balanced diet that includes waterfowl pellets, grains, and vegetables. Avoid relying solely on bread or unhealthy treats, as this can lead to nutritional imbalances.

Grit: Ducks need access to grit, such as small stones, to aid in digestion. Grit helps grind down food in their gizzard, improving their overall digestion.

Nutritional Supplements: Consult a veterinarian to determine if your ducks need additional vitamins or minerals, especially during stages like egg laying. A proper diet is crucial for their overall health and egg production.

Egg Laying Issues

Nesting Boxes: Provide comfortable and secure nesting boxes with clean bedding for your ducks to lay their eggs. A conducive nesting area reduces stress and encourages consistent egg-laying.

Egg Eating: Collect eggs frequently to prevent ducks from pecking and breaking them. Provide clean and comfortable nesting boxes to discourage egg-eating behavior.

Feeding Considerations

Adjustment: Modify the amount of food based on your ducks' age, size, and activity level. Avoid overfeeding, which can lead to obesity and related health issues.

Molting

Nutrition: During molting, ducks require extra nutrients for healthy feather regrowth. Make sure they receive a nutrient-rich diet to support this natural process.

Temperature Regulation

Hot Weather: Ducks can struggle in hot weather. Provide shade, cool water, and proper ventilation to help them stay comfortable. Avoid heat stress by monitoring their behavior.

Cold Weather: Ducks are more susceptible to cold in wet conditions. Insulate their shelter and provide adequate bedding to keep them warm during colder months.

Foot and Leg Health

Clean Bedding: Provide clean bedding to prevent foot infections. Regularly inspect your ducks' feet for cuts, sores, or signs of bumblefoot, which is a bacterial infection.

Social Dynamics

Observation: Watch for signs of bullying or isolation within the flock. If necessary, separate aggressive ducks to prevent stress and injuries.

Quarantine

New Ducks: Quarantine new ducks before introducing them to your existing flock. This prevents the potential spread of diseases.

Hygiene Practices

Cleanliness: Wash your hands after handling ducks or cleaning their environment to prevent the transmission of germs. Regularly disinfect equipment and tools you use for their care.

Routine Health Checks

Observation: Establish a routine for observing your ducks' overall health. Look for any changes in behavior, appetite, or physical condition that could indicate a health issue.

Interaction and Enrichment

Bonding: Spend time interacting with your ducks to build trust and strengthen your bond. Hand-feeding treats or simply spending time nearby can foster a positive relationship.

Enrichment: Provide environmental enrichment such as toys, shallow pools, and hiding spots to keep your ducks mentally stimulated and engaged.

Frequently Asked Questions

Egg Care

Q: How can you prevent egg eating in ducks?

A: To do that, provide clean and comfortable nesting boxes with sufficient bedding. Collect eggs promptly and consider using fake ones to discourage pecking.

Egg eating can become a habit if not addressed promptly. Ducks may accidentally break an egg and then learn to eat the contents. To prevent this behavior, create inviting nesting boxes with clean straw or bedding where ducks feel secure laying eggs. Collecting eggs frequently reduces the opportunity for ducks to peck at and consume them. Using fake eggs or golf balls in the nests can deter pecking behavior by providing an unappetizing experience.

Integrating Ducks

Q: How can you integrate new ducks into an existing flock?

A: Gradually introducing new ducks helps reduce stress and aggression. Initially, keep the new ducks separated but within sight of the existing flock initially. After a period of observation, allow supervised interactions to establish a pecking order. Provide hiding spots and multiple feeding stations to reduce competition and bullying.

Integrating new ducks into an existing flock requires a thoughtful approach to minimize stress and potential conflicts. Ducks are social animals but establish a pecking order that can lead to initial tensions. By allowing the new ducks to see and hear the existing flock before direct contact, you reduce the shock of introduction. Supervised interactions in a neutral space allow ducks to establish their hierarchy without severe aggression. Providing hiding spots and multiple food and water sources ensures that new and existing ducks have enough resources, reducing the risk of bullying and promoting a smoother integration process.

Winter Care
Q: How do you keep ducks warm in winter?

A: Insulate the duck shelter using straw, hay, or other suitable materials to provide warmth. Ensure proper ventilation to prevent moisture buildup, which can lead to frostbite. Ducks generate body heat, so huddling together can help keep them warm. Provide ample bedding, offer access to clean, unfrozen water, and protect them from drafts.

Ducks are more cold-hardy than they might appear, but providing appropriate winter care is important for their comfort and health. Insulating their shelter with materials like straw or hay traps heat and creates a warmer environment. Adequate ventilation prevents excessive humidity and moisture buildup, which can lead to frostbite and respiratory issues. Ducks tend to huddle together for warmth, so provide enough space and bedding for them to do so comfortably. Offering access to clean and unfrozen water is crucial for hydration and overall well-being. Preventing drafts and providing a snug and insulated shelter contribute to your ducks' ability to withstand colder temperatures.

Vaccinations
Q: Do ducks need vaccinations?

A: While ducks typically don't require routine vaccinations, consult a poultry veterinarian for recommendations based on your specific location and circumstances. Vaccinations can vary by region and disease prevalence.

The need for vaccinations in ducks varies depending on factors such as your region and the prevalence of specific diseases. Ducks are generally resilient birds, but certain diseases can impact their health and egg production. Consulting a poultry veterinarian with knowledge of local disease risks can determine if vaccinations are necessary to protect your ducks. Regular veterinary care, proper nutrition, and a clean living environment are key components of maintaining the health and well-being of your ducks.

Sexing Ducks

Q: How can you tell if your ducks are male or female?

A: Sexing ducks can be challenging, especially in some breeds. While males (drakes) often have curled tail feathers and females (ducks) have a more subtle quack, accurate sex determination might require professional expertise or DNA testing.

Sexing ducks can be difficult, especially when they're young. In some breeds, males and females have distinct visual differences, such as curled tail feathers in males and a more subdued quack in females. However, these indicators might not be foolproof, and variations can occur. Professional expertise or DNA testing is often the most accurate way to determine the sex of ducks. Some physical and behavioral differences may become more apparent as ducks mature, but relying solely on visual cues can lead to misidentifications.

Broody Ducks

Q: What do you do if your duck becomes broody?

A: Broodiness is a natural behavior where ducks sit on eggs to hatch them. If you're not interested in hatching eggs, gently discourage this behavior by promptly removing eggs. You can also offer distractions and consider isolating the broody duck for a short time.

Broodiness is an instinctual behavior where ducks want to incubate and hatch eggs. While this behavior is natural, it may not always be convenient if you're not interested in raising ducklings. To discourage broodiness, remove eggs from the nest as soon as possible. This prevents the duck from becoming too attached to the eggs and decreases the likelihood of successful incubation. Offering distractions like changing the nest location or providing new bedding can also break the broody cycle. If needed, you can isolate the broody duck in a separate area for a few days to redirect her focus.

Egg Laying

Q: When do ducks start laying eggs?

A: Ducks typically start laying eggs around 5-7 months of age, but this can vary based on factors such as breed, environmental conditions, and nutrition.

The age at which ducks start laying eggs depends on multiple factors. Most will begin laying between 5 and 7 months old, but this can vary widely based on breed and individual differences. Providing appropriate nutrition and ensuring a stress-free environment can encourage earlier and more consistent egg laying. Factors such as daylight duration and temperature can also influence egg production. By monitoring their behavior and providing proper care, you can ensure your ducks have a successful egg-laying season.

Duckling Care

Q: How do you care for ducklings?

A: Ducklings require a warm and safe environment. Use a brooder with a heat lamp to maintain the right temperature. Provide waters that are shallow and accessible for them to drink and clean themselves. Feed them a starter diet formulated specifically for ducklings.

Ducklings are delicate and require attentive care during their early stages of life. A brooder provides a controlled environment where temperature is crucial. A heat lamp or heating pad ensures that ducklings stay warm, as they cannot regulate their body temperature effectively. Shallow waters prevent accidental drowning. Ducklings need access to clean water for drinking and cleaning themselves. Starter diets for ducklings are specially formulated to provide the necessary nutrients for growth and development. Their nutritional requirements will change as they mature, so it's important to adjust their diet accordingly. Proper care and nutrition during the duckling stage set the foundation for healthy growth and adulthood.

Egg Incubation

Q: Can you incubate duck eggs without a mother duck?

A: Yes, you can incubate duck eggs artificially using an incubator. Maintain proper temperature and humidity levels as specified for the duck egg breed. Turning the eggs several times a day is crucial for successful hatching.

Artificial incubation allows you to hatch duck eggs without the presence of a broody duck. An incubator replicates the conditions needed for successful egg development and hatching. Maintaining consistent temperature and humidity levels is essential, as these factors influence embryo development and hatch rates. Different duck breeds may have specific requirements, so it's important to research and adjust settings accordingly. Turning the eggs multiple times daily prevents the embryo from sticking to the shell and promotes even development. Proper incubation techniques and careful monitoring and adjustments increase the chances of a successful hatch and healthy ducklings.

Feather Plucking

Q: Why do ducks sometimes pluck each other's feathers?

A: Feather plucking can result from overcrowding, stress, boredom, or nutritional deficiencies. To minimize feather plucking, make sure they have enough space, offer mental stimulation, and provide a balanced diet.

Various factors can cause feather plucking. Overcrowding in the coop or lack of space can lead to stress and aggression among ducks, resulting in feather plucking. Boredom and lack of mental stimulation can also contribute to this behavior. Ducks may engage in feather plucking if they have nutritional deficiencies or if their diet lacks essential nutrients. To prevent feather plucking, make sure that ducks have enough space to move around and interact without feeling crowded. Provide mental stimulation via toys, mirrors, and items to peck at to keep them engaged. Offering a balanced and nutritious diet tailored to their needs minimizes the risk of nutritional deficiencies that may lead to feather plucking.

Egg-Laying Patterns

Q: How often do ducks lay eggs?

A: Egg-laying frequency varies depending on factors such as breed, age, and lighting conditions. On average, ducks lay eggs every 24-26 hours. Some may lay consistently, while others may do so intermittently.

Ducks' egg-laying patterns can vary widely based on individual characteristics and environmental factors. Different breeds have different levels of egg production, with some being more prolific layers than others. Age also plays a role, as younger ducks tend to lay more eggs than older ones. Lighting conditions, particularly the number of daylight hours, influence egg production. Ducks typically lay eggs every 24-26 hours, with most laying early in the morning. However, some ducks may lay intermittently or take breaks from egg production. Monitoring egg-laying patterns and providing proper care, including suitable lighting, ensures optimal egg production and overall well-being.

Duck Sounds

Q: What do duck sounds mean?

A: Ducks communicate through various sounds. For example, females typically have a quack, while males make softer sounds. Quacking can indicate excitement, warning of danger, or simply socializing. Observing their behavior alongside sounds will help you understand their communication.

Ducks use vocalizations to communicate a range of messages and emotions. The quack is one of the most recognizable duck sounds and is typically associated with females. Male ducks often make softer sounds or whistles. Quacking can indicate excitement, such as when ducks are anticipating feeding or swimming. It can also serve as a warning signal to alert other ducks to potential danger. Ducks quack to maintain social connections and establish their presence within the flock. Observing their behavior and the context of their vocalizations will help you interpret their communication and understand their needs and feelings.

Molting

Q: How long does molting typically last?

A: Molting is the process of shedding old feathers and growing new ones. It can last several weeks to a couple of months. Provide proper nutrition and care during this time to support healthy feather regrowth.

Molting typically occurs annually and lasts from several weeks to a few months. During this time, ducks may look scruffy, and their egg production may decrease or cease temporarily. Molting requires significant energy, so providing a balanced and nutrient-rich diet is crucial to support healthy feather regrowth. Ducks may be more susceptible to stress and predation during molting, so make sure they have a safe and comfortable environment during this period. Once molting is complete, ducks will have fresh feathers that contribute to their overall health and appearance.

Duck Health and Medications

Q: Can you use medications on ducks that are intended for chickens?

A: Some safe medications for chickens may not be suitable for ducks. Always consult a poultry veterinarian before administering any medications to ensure proper dosage and effectiveness.

While chickens and ducks are both poultry, they have distinct physiological differences that can impact how they metabolize medications. Medications that are safe for chickens may not necessarily be safe or effective for ducks. Some may have different dosages, withdrawal periods, or potential side effects when used in ducks. Consulting a poultry veterinarian with experience in duck care is essential. A professional can provide guidance on appropriate treatments and dosages to ensure the health and well-being of your ducks.

Duck Behavior

Q: Why do ducks shake their heads in the water?

A: Ducks shake their heads in the water to clean their bills, eyes, and nostrils. This behavior helps remove dirt and debris, keeping their sensitive areas clean.

Ducks shake their heads as a natural behavior to maintain hygiene and comfort. When they do it in the water, they're cleaning their bills, eyes, and nostrils. They use their bills to forage for food and interact with their environment, so keeping them clean is important for overall health. Head shaking helps remove dirt, debris, and any foreign particles that may have accumulated. By observing this behavior, you can witness ducks' natural self-care routines and their adaptations for staying clean and healthy.

Duck Adoption

Q: Can you adopt or rescue ducks?

A: Yes, you can adopt or rescue ducks in need. Contact animal shelters, rescue organizations, or farm animal sanctuaries to inquire about adopting ducks. Make sure you can provide the appropriate care and living conditions before adopting.

Adopting or rescuing ducks can be a rewarding experience, but it requires careful consideration and preparation. If you want to provide a home for ducks in need, contact local animal shelters, rescue organizations, or farm animal sanctuaries. Due to various circumstances, such as abandonment or owner surrender, these organizations may have ducks available for adoption. You need to have the necessary resources, space, and knowledge to provide proper care. Ducks have specific needs, and it's important to create a suitable and safe environment that meets their requirements for housing, nutrition, and overall well-being.

These frequently asked questions provide valuable insights into the world of duck-keeping. By understanding and addressing these topics, you'll be better equipped to provide optimal care for your ducks and create a fulfilling and enriching experience for both you and your feathered companions.

Conclusion

There are so many reasons to consider opting for ducks over chickens or even alongside them. Ducks are known for their friendly nature, and caring for them can bring a lot of enjoyment. However, you should understand the responsibilities that come with duck care and what you should and shouldn't do.

Here are some key takeaways: Ducks don't require an elaborate shelter. They prefer a shelter with a bit of breeze and some moisture. It also needs to be predator-proof because of the many potential threats ducks face. Additionally, it should ideally be at ground level or close to it, as most ducks are uncomfortable with elevation.

Ducks need water, both for drinking and swimming. Creating a small pond is not necessary. As long as ducks can swim in a circle, they'll be content spending a significant part of their day doing so.

When selecting a duck type, choose one that suits your needs and is manageable for you. While getting fresh eggs daily is rewarding, keep in mind that two people with just four ducks could yield up to 800 eggs annually.

Caring for and interacting with ducks can be enjoyable, but it's a commitment that requires proper knowledge of feeding and care. This guide provides you with enough information to help you create a suitable habitat for your ducks, ensuring their well-being and happiness. Start small, especially if you're raising ducks for your personal use. If you have access to clean water nearby, your ducks can thrive.

Remember that even the quietest ducks can generate some noise and tend to be early risers. If you have neighbors, consider their comfort. Additionally, make sure to check with local authorities to confirm whether you're allowed to keep ducks and if there are any limits on the number you can keep.

On the flip side, ducks have charming personalities. They're curious, affectionate, and can become quite attached to their human caregivers. You're in for a treat if you're raising them for eggs. Duck eggs are larger and richer than chicken eggs, making them a prized ingredient in the kitchen. Plus, ducks are nature's pest control experts. They'll happily munch on slugs, snails, and various insects, which can help keep your garden pest-free. They also offer the bonus of feathers and down, which can be harvested for various craft projects or even sold. Beyond the practical benefits, raising ducks can deepen your connection to the natural world. It's a hands-on way to appreciate the cycles of life, the changing seasons, and the simple joys of outdoor living.

Here's another book by Dion Rosser that you might like

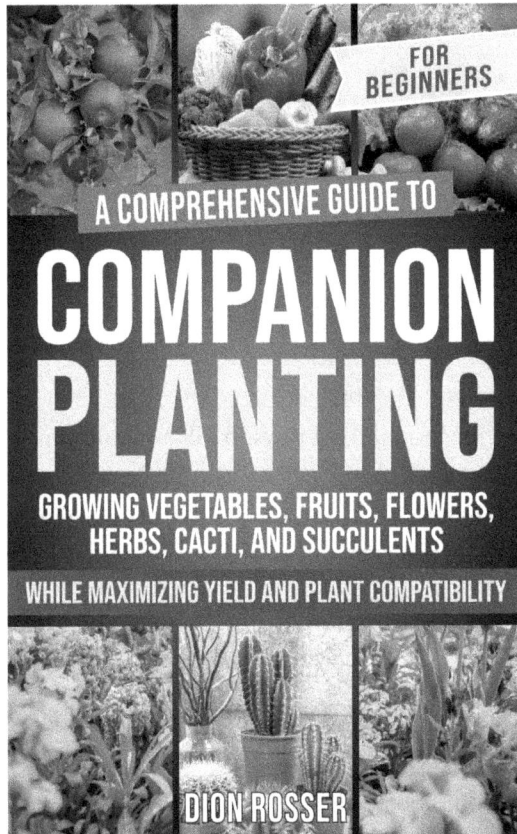

FOR BEGINNERS

A COMPREHENSIVE GUIDE TO

COMPANION PLANTING

GROWING VEGETABLES, FRUITS, FLOWERS, HERBS, CACTI, AND SUCCULENTS

WHILE MAXIMIZING YIELD AND PLANT COMPATIBILITY

DION ROSSER

References

(2008, March 20). Ethical breeding: 10 golden rules. Tru-Luv Rabbitry: Quality Holland Lops in Malaysia. https://truluvrabbitry.com/2008/03/20/ethical-breeding-10-golden-rules/

(2021, February 1). Slaughter: how animals are killed. Viva! The Vegan Charity; Viva! https://viva.org.uk/animals/slaughter-how-animals-are-killed/

(N.d.). Fao.org. https://www.fao.org/3/t1690e/t1690e.pdf

(n.d.). Killing rabbits for food. 3 best ways to kill a rabbit. Raising-rabbits.com. https://www.raising-rabbits.com/killing-rabbits.html

(n.d.). Recommended methods of euthanasia: Rabbits. Umaryland.edu. https://www.umaryland.edu/media/umb/oaa/oac/oawa/guidelines/Euthanasia_Rabbits_12.2020.pdf

(n.d.). Slaughtering and dressing rabbits. Msstate.edu. http://extension.msstate.edu/content/slaughtering-and-dressing-rabbits

(N.d.). Standardmedia.Co.Ke. https://www.standardmedia.co.ke/farmkenya/amp/article/2001340660/how-to-make-better-use-of-rabbits-by-products%2010

10 of the most common rabbit health emergencies. (2020, April 16). Best4Bunny. https://www.best4bunny.com/10-of-the-most-common-rabbit-health-emergencies/

Alyssa. (2019, November 4). What do you get from a meat rabbit? Homestead Rabbits. https://homesteadrabbits.com/meat-rabbit-parts/

Alyssa. (2019, October 11). Commercial meat rabbit growth rates. Homestead Rabbits. https://homesteadrabbits.com/meat-rabbit-growth-rates/

Alyssa. (2022, March 4). Raise Meat Rabbits: Quick start guide. Homestead Rabbits. https://homesteadrabbits.com/raise-meat-rabbits/

Alyssa. (2022, March 4). Raise Meat Rabbits: Quick start guide. Homestead Rabbits. https://homesteadrabbits.com/raise-meat-rabbits/

Baby rabbit information. (n.d.). Com.au. https://mtmarthavet.com.au/baby-rabbit-information/

Barnett, T. (2020, April 13). Can you keep rabbits outdoors: Tips for raising backyard rabbits. Gardening Know How. https://www.gardeningknowhow.com/garden-how-to/beneficial/can-you-keep-rabbits-outdoors.htm

Brad. (2021, January 3). Flemish Giant Rabbits: Care and Breeding. Northern Nester. https://northernnester.com/flemish-giant-rabbits/

Browning, H., & Veit, W. (2020). Is humane slaughter possible? Animals: An Open Access Journal from MDPI, 10(5), 799. https://doi.org/10.3390/ani10050799

Budnick, T. (n.d.). A "hare" raising lapse in meat industry regulation: How regulatory reform will pull the meat rabbit out from welfare neglect. Animallaw.Info. https://www.animallaw.info/sites/default/files/Rabbit%20Meat%20%26%20Regulatory%20Reform.pdf

Californian rabbit characteristics, origin, uses. (2022, January 31). ROYS FARM. https://www.roysfarm.com/californian-rabbit/

Caring for an older rabbit. (n.d.). Org.uk. https://www.rspca.org.uk/adviceandwelfare/pets/rabbits/senior

Carter, L. (2020, May 3). How to take care of baby bunnies. Rabbit Care Tips; Lou Carter. https://www.rabbitcaretips.com/how-to-take-care-of-baby-bunnies/

Code of practice for the intensive husbandry of rabbits. (2020, June 23). Agriculture Victoria. https://agriculture.vic.gov.au/livestock-and-animals/animal-welfare-victoria/pocta-act-1986/victorian-codes-of-practice-for-animal-welfare/code-of-practice-for-the-intensive-husbandry-of-rabbits

Collaborator, B. (2020, January 30). What temperature is too cold for rabbits? K&H Pet Products. https://khpet.com/blogs/small-animals/what-temperature-is-too-cold-for-rabbits

Creating a good home for rabbits. (n.d.). Org.uk. https://www.rspca.org.uk/adviceandwelfare/pets/rabbits/environment

Creating the ideal home for your rabbits. (n.d.-b). Org.uk. https://www.pdsa.org.uk/pet-help-and-advice/looking-after-your-pet/rabbits/creating-the-ideal-home-for-your-rabbits

Crossbreeding, outcrossing, linebreeding, and inbreeding. (n.d.). LOTS OF LOPS RABBITRY. http://www.lotsoflops.com/crossbreeding-outcrossing-linebreeding-and-inbreeding.html

Dec. (2017, December 21). Five common diseases that affect rabbits. Petmd.com; PetMD. https://www.petmd.com/rabbit/conditions/five-common-diseases-affect-rabbits

Diina, N. (n.d.). Farm4Trade Suite. Farm4tradesuite.com. https://www.farm4tradesuite.com/blog/10-reasons-to-start-raising-rabbits

Flemish Giant rabbit: Characteristics, uses, origin. (2022, January 31). ROYS FARM. https://www.roysfarm.com/flemish-giant-rabbit/

Guidelines for keeping pet rabbits. (2020, June 12). Agriculture Victoria. https://agriculture.vic.gov.au/livestock-and-animals/animal-welfare-victoria/other-pets/rabbits/guidelines-for-keeping-pet-rabbits

How to skin a rabbit: 2 easy methods (with pictures). (2009, May 2). WikiHow. https://www.wikihow.com/Skin-a-Rabbit

Humane slaughter: how we reduce animal suffering. (2014, May 27). World Animal Protection.

Is rabbit manure good to use in the garden? (2020, July 15). Deep Green Permaculture. https://deepgreenpermaculture.com/2020/07/15/is-rabbit-manure-good-to-use-in-the-garden/?amp=1

Jollity. (2020, February 7). Rabbit lifespan and life stages. Oxbow Animal Health. https://oxbowanimalhealth.com/blog/rabbit-life-stages/

Jones, O. (2020, April 15). 10 best meat rabbit breeds in the world (2023 update). Pet Keen. https://petkeen.com/best-meat-rabbit-breeds/

Kathryn. (2013, December 23). Colony raising rabbits: How to get started. Farming My Backyard. https://farmingmybackyard.com/colonyraisingrabbits101/

Kathryn. (2013, December 23). Colony raising rabbits: How to get started. Farming My Backyard. https://farmingmybackyard.com/colonyraisingrabbits101/

Kathryn. (2019, December 12). Which meat rabbit breeds should you raise? Farming My Backyard. https://farmingmybackyard.com/meat-rabbit-breeds/

Kathryn. (2019, May 29). The best ways to feed rabbits (besides pellets)! Farming My Backyard. https://farmingmybackyard.com/feed-rabbits/

Kellogg, K. (2022, January 4). How to tan a rabbit hide. Mother Earth News – The Original Guide To Living Wisely; Mother Earth News. https://www.motherearthnews.com/diy/how-to-tan-a-rabbit-hide-zmaz83jfzraw/

Klopp, J. (n.d.). Bunny Farming: Why Do People Farm Rabbits? Is It Cruel? Thehumaneleague.org. https://thehumaneleague.org/article/bunny-farming

Kruesi, G. (2020, January 3). Staying warm with rabbit wool. Chelsea Green Publishing. https://www.chelseagreen.com/2020/staying-warm-with-rabbit-wool/

Martin, A. (n.d.). Caring for the elderly or senior rabbit. Lafeber.com. https://lafeber.com/mammals/caring-for-the-elderly-or-senior-rabbit/

McClure, D. (n.d.). Disorders and Diseases of Rabbits. MSD Veterinary Manual. https://www.msdvetmanual.com/all-other-pets/rabbits/disorders-and-diseases-of-rabbits

Montano, C. (2021, January 18). Bone Broth or rabbit. Christinamontano.com. https://www.christinamontano.com/amp/bone-broth-or-rabbit

Murphree, M. E. (n.d.). Backyard grower-consumer perceptions of rabbit meat consumption in rural Mississippi al Mississippi. Msstate.edu. https://scholarsjunction.msstate.edu/cgi/viewcontent.cgi?article=6542&context=td

Ned, & Hannah. (2023, February 13). 6 surprising rabbit manure benefits. The Making Life. https://themakinglife.com/rabbit-manure-benefits/

New Zealand rabbit characteristics use origin. (2022, January 31). ROYS FARM. https://www.roysfarm.com/new-zealand-rabbit/

NOSE TO TAIL-uses for every part of the domestic rabbit. (2012, February 11). Rise and Shine Rabbitry. https://riseandshinerabbitry.com/2012/02/11/nose-to-tail-uses-for-every-part-of-the-domestic-rabbit/

Ockert, K. (2015, November 10). MSU extension. MSU Extension. https://www.canr.msu.edu/news/determining_cage_size_for_rabbits

Owuor, S. A., Mamati, E. G., & Kasili, R. W. (2019). Origin, genetic diversity, and population structure of rabbits (Oryctolagus cuniculus) in Kenya. BioMed Research International, 2019, 7056940. https://doi.org/10.1155/2019/7056940

Pellets and nutrition for meat rabbits. (2012, May 23). Rise and Shine Rabbitry. https://riseandshinerabbitry.com/2012/05/23/pellets-and-nutrition-for-meat-rabbits/

Peoria zoo. (2014, April 7). Peoria Zoo. https://www.peoriazoo.org/animal-groups/mammals/giant-flemish-rabbit/

Planning a Homemade Rabbit Cage. (2014). Therabbithouse.com. http://www.therabbithouse.com/indoor/designing-rabbit-cage.asp

Poindexter, J. (2017, February 23). How to butcher a rabbit humanely in 6 quick and easy steps. Morning Chores. https://morningchores.com/how-to-butcher-a-rabbit/

Pratt, A. (2019, November 11). 5 life stages of pet rabbits and how to keep them healthy. The Bunny Lady; Amy Pratt. https://bunnylady.com/rabbit-life-stages/

Pratt, A. (2020, March 6). How to make Critical Care rabbit formula for emergencies. The Bunny Lady; Amy Pratt. https://bunnylady.com/critical-care/

Pratt, A. (2021, April 5). Rabbits need more space than you think. The Bunny Lady; Amy Pratt. https://bunnylady.com/space-for-rabbits/

Pratt, A. (2021, March 8). How big do rabbits get? (smallest and largest breeds). The Bunny Lady; Amy Pratt. https://bunnylady.com/how-big-do-rabbits-get/

Preparing for emergencies. (n.d.). Therabbithaven.org. https://therabbithaven.org/preparing-for-emergencies

Rabbit bones. (n.d.). Steaksandgame.com. https://www.steaksandgame.com/rabbit-bones-1458

Rabbit breeding system. (2020, April 12). McGreen Acres. https://mcgreenacres.com/blog/rabbits/rabbit-breeding-system

Rabbit breeds: Best 17 for highest profits. (2022, January 28). ROYS FARM. https://www.roysfarm.com/rabbit-breeds/

Rabbit farming: Best beginner's guide with 28 tips. (2022, January 7). ROYS FARM. https://www.roysfarm.com/rabbit-farming/

Rabbit personalities and lifespan. (n.d.). The Anti-Cruelty Society. https://anticruelty.org/pet-library/rabbit-personalities-and-lifespan

Rabbit stock. (2008, January 28). Saveur. https://www.saveur.com/article/Recipes/Rabbit-Stock/

Rabbit's life cycle: From bunny to adult. (n.d.). CYHY. https://creatureyearstohumanyears.com/resources/rabbit-life-cycle

Raising meat rabbits. (2016, October 14). Farming My Backyard. https://farmingmybackyard.com/rabbits/

Richardson, H. (2022, June 8). How to know when to cull rabbits. Everbreed. https://everbreed.com/blog/how-to-know-when-to-cull-rabbits/

Shy rabbits. (2011, July 10). House Rabbit Society. https://rabbit.org/2011/07/faq-shy-rabbits/

Składanowska-Baryza, J., Ludwiczak, A., Pruszyńska-Oszmałek, E., Kołodziejski, P., & Stanisz, M. (2020). Effect of two different stunning methods on the quality traits of rabbit meat. Animals: An Open Access Journal from MDPI, 10(4), 700. https://doi.org/10.3390/ani10040700 (72), K. (2018, September 18). How to skin a rabbit – A step-by-step guide. Steemit. https://steemit.com/howto/@ketcom/how-to-skin-a-rabbit-a-step-by-step-guide

Suitable environment for rabbits. (2015, November 20). Nidirect. https://www.nidirect.gov.uk/articles/suitable-environment-rabbits

Sullivan, K. (2019, November 26). Is your rabbit sick? 9 signs the answer may be "yes." PETA. https://www.peta.org/living/animal-companions/is-my-rabbit-sick/

Tertitsa, T. (2013, October 27). Rabbit stewardship: Ethical, humane, conscientious raising/husbandry. One Community Global. https://www.onecommunityglobal.org/rabbits/

The Backyard Rabbitry. (2023, February 6). How to choose the right rabbit breed for meat production. The Backyard Rabbitry. https://thebackyardrabbitry.com/how-to/how-to-choose-the-right-rabbit-breed-for-meat-production.html

Vanderzanden, E., & Kerr, S. (n.d.). Raising rabbits for meat: Providing basic care. Oregonstate.edu. https://catalog.extension.oregonstate.edu/sites/catalog/files/project/pdf/ec1655.pdf

Vanderzanden, E., & Kerr, S. (n.d.). Raising rabbits for meat: Providing basic care. Oregonstate.edu. https://catalog.extension.oregonstate.edu/sites/catalog/files/project/pdf/ec1655.pdf

Walker, J. (2015, January 29). Keeping pregnant rabbits healthy, safe and warm. Coops and Cages. https://www.coopsandcages.com.au/blog/keep-pregnant-rabbits-safe-healthy-warm/

What to feed meat rabbits. (2019, February 14). Countryside. https://www.iamcountryside.com/homesteading/feed-meat-rabbits/

What to know about New Zealand rabbits. (n.d.). WebMD. https://www.webmd.com/pets/what-to-know-about-new-zealand-rabbits

What to know about the Californian rabbit. (n.d.). WebMD. https://www.webmd.com/pets/what-to-know-about-californian-rabbits

What to know about the Flemish giant rabbit. (n.d.). WebMD. https://www.webmd.com/pets/flemish-giant-rabbit

(N.d.). Bothellwa.gov. https://www.bothellwa.gov/561/Dont-Feed-the-Birds#:~:text=A%3A%20Ducks%20are%20natural%20foragers,plants%2C%20crustaceans%2C%20and%20more.

(N.d.). Veterinariadigital.com. https://www.veterinariadigital.com/en/articulos/main-challenges-in-duck-production/

(N.d.-a). Pethelpful.com. https://pethelpful.com/birds/Keeping-Pet-Ducks-and-Geese

(N.d.-b). Zendesk.com. https://meyerhatchery.zendesk.com/hc/en-us/articles/5316673386509-Raising-Ducks-for-Meat#:~:text=For%20the%20first%204%20weeks,not%20gain%20weight%20as%20efficiently.

12 reasons why duck eggs are better than chicken eggs. (2019, November 12). Fresh Eggs Daily® with Lisa Steele. https://www.fresheggsdaily.blog/2019/11/duck-eggs-vs-chicken-eggs-12-reasons.html

Accetta-Scott, A. (2021, October 27). Selecting the best ducks for eggs. Backyard Poultry. https://backyardpoultry.iamcountryside.com/poultry-101/selecting-the-best-ducks-for-eggs/

Addison, J. (2023, May 2). Feeding Ducks: The best food to keep ducks healthy & happy. Birds & Wetlands. https://birdsandwetlands.com/feeding-ducks/

Affeld, M. (2019, November 21). 10 delectable duck egg recipes. Insteading. https://insteading.com/blog/duck-egg-recipes/

Aktar, W., Sengupta, D., & Chowdhury, A. (2009). Impact of pesticides use in agriculture: their benefits and hazards. Interdisciplinary Toxicology, 2(1), 1–12. https://doi.org/10.2478/v10102-009-0001-7

American Pekin duck characteristics, origin, uses. (2021, May 31). ROYS FARM. https://www.roysfarm.com/pekin-duck/

Ariane Helmbrecht. (n.d.). Presswarehouse.com. https://styluspub.presswarehouse.com/browse/author/ff544176-aca6-4453-8b46-b9c9b67db340/Helmbrecht-Ariane

Aylesbury duck characteristics, origin & uses info. (2021, May 31). ROYS FARM. https://www.roysfarm.com/aylesbury-duck/

Aylesbury ducks: Complete breed guide. (n.d.). Fowl Guide. https://fowlguide.com/aylesbury-ducks/

Backyard Sidekick. (2022, October 6). Why do ducks quack? The various meanings of duck quacks. Backyard Sidekick. https://backyardsidekick.com/why-do-ducks-quack-the-various-meanings-of-duck-quacks/

Badgett, B. (2019, August 2). Duck habitat safety – what are some plants ducks can't eat. Gardening Know How. https://www.gardeningknowhow.com/garden-how-to/beneficial/plants-ducks-cant-eat.htm

Barnes, A. (2019, May 15). Daily diet, treats, and supplements for ducks. The Open Sanctuary Project; The Open Sanctuary Project, Inc. https://opensanctuary.org/daily-diet-treats-and-supplements-for-ducks/

Batres-Marquez, S.P. (2017, June 29). U.S. duck production and exports. Iowafarmbureau.com. https://www.iowafarmbureau.com/Article/US-Duck-Production-and-Exports

Bauer, E. (n.d.). Chocolate Mousse. Simply Recipes. https://www.simplyrecipes.com/recipes/chocolate_mousse/

Bethany. (2021, August 30). Raising baby ducks for beginners. Homesteading Where You Are. https://www.homesteadingwhereyouare.com/2021/08/30/raising-baby-ducks-for-beginners/

Bethany. (2022, February 4). All about niacin for ducks: What you should know. Homesteading Where You Are. https://www.homesteadingwhereyouare.com/2022/02/03/niacin-for-ducks/

Brahlek, A. (n.d.). A guide to the ideal diet for backyard ducks. Grubblyfarms.com. https://grubblyfarms.com/blogs/the-flyer/backyard-ducks-diet

Campbell, V. (2015, January 20). How to recognize duck courtship displays. All About Birds. https://www.allaboutbirds.org/news/what-to-watch-for-duck-courtship-video/

Can ducks eat chicken feed? Duck feeding 101. (2020, August 22). Rural Living Today. https://rurallivingtoday.com/backyard-chickens-roosters/can-ducks-eat-chicken-feed/

Chaussee, R. (n.d.). Amino acid nutrition in ducks. Org.Br.

Chiou, J. (2021, September 16). Caramelized apple French toast. Table for Two® by Julie Chiou; Table for Two. https://www.tablefortwoblog.com/caramelized-apple-french-toast/

Commercial feeds. (2012, July 24). Horse Sport. https://horsesport.com/magazine/nutrition/commercial-feeds/

Cosgrove, N. (2022, August 5). Indian runner duck: Pictures, info, traits & care guide. Pet Keen. https://petkeen.com/indian-runner-duck/

DeVore, S. (2020, May 3). Duck breeds. Farminence. https://farminence.com/duck-breeds/

Dickson, P. (2022, October 1). Do ducks purr? Bird noises & interesting facts. Pet Keen. https://petkeen.com/do-ducks-purr/

Diet requirements for backyard ducks - A comprehensive guide. (2023, February 23). Sharpes Stock Feeds; Sharpes Stockfeed. https://www.stockfeed.co.nz/resources/poultry-feed/ducks-diet-requirements/

Dodrill, T. (2021, December 10). Duck language: How to interpret duck behavior. New Life On A Homestead. https://www.newlifeonahomestead.com/duck-language-and-behavior/

Duck egg production, lighting, and incubation. (2021). Gov.au. https://www.dpi.nsw.gov.au/animals-and-livestock/poultry-and-birds/species/duck-raising/egg-production

Duck eggs —. (n.d.). Orange Star Farm. https://www.orangestarfarm.com/duck-eggs

Duck health care. (2020, February 13). Cornell University College of Veterinary Medicine. https://www.vet.cornell.edu/animal-health-diagnostic-center/programs/duck-research-lab/health-care

Duck nutrition. (2020, February 17). Cornell University College of Veterinary Medicine. https://www.vet.cornell.edu/animal-health-diagnostic-center/programs/duck-research-lab/duck-nutrition

Emily. (2022, April 22). Duck egg quiche. This Healthy Table. https://thishealthytable.com/blog/duck-egg-quiche/

Feed mixers for cattle, poultry & Co – amixon® blog. (n.d.). Amixon.com. https://www.amixon.com/en/blog/feed-mixers

Feed supplements poultry shellgrit, Packaging Type: Bags. (n.d.). Indiamart.com. https://www.indiamart.com/proddetail/shellgrit-10716078848.html

Feeding ducks. (n.d.). Ncsu.edu. https://poultry.ces.ncsu.edu/backyard-flocks-eggs/other-fowl/feeding-ducks/

Ferraro-Fanning, A. (2022, June 21). Duck-safe plants and weeds from the garden. Backyard Poultry. https://backyardpoultry.iamcountryside.com/poultry-101/weeding-the-garden-and-duck-safe-plants/

Fraser, C. (2022, May 17). Pekin duck (American Pekin): Pictures, info, traits, & care guide. Pet Keen. https://petkeen.com/pekin-duck/

Girl, L. E. D. (2012, May 31). The beginner's guide to hatching duck eggs. Fresh Eggs Daily® with Lisa Steele. https://www.fresheggsdaily.blog/2012/05/great-eggscape-too-hatching-duck-eggs.html

Greer, T. (2020, July 6). How much protein do ducks really need? Morning Chores. https://morningchores.com/protein-requirements-for-ducks/

Gregory. (2021, July 23). Duck eggs: Taste, preparation, shelf life, and more. Fowl Guide. https://fowlguide.com/duck-eggs-taste-preparation/

HappyChicken. (2020, September 26). Interpreting duck behavior. The Happy Chicken Coop. https://www.thehappychickencoop.com/interpreting-duck-behavior/

HappyChicken. (2021, October 12). Pekin duck breed: Everything you need to know. The Happy Chicken Coop. https://www.thehappychickencoop.com/pekin-duck-breed-everything-you-need-to-know/

HappyChicken. (2022, March 2). Ducks need water. The Happy Chicken Coop. https://www.thehappychickencoop.com/do-ducks-need-water-what-you-should-know/

HappyChicken. (2022, March 4). Best meat duck breeds. The Happy Chicken Coop. https://www.thehappychickencoop.com/best-meat-duck-breeds/

Health & Social Services. (n.d.). Duck. Gov.Nt.Ca. https://www.hss.gov.nt.ca/en/services/nutritional-food-fact-sheet-series/duck

Henke, J. (2020, August 3). Should you wash eggs or not? Successful Farming. https://www.agriculture.com/podcast/living-the-country-life-radio/should-you-wash-eggs-or-not

Herlihy, S. (2022, June 6). Khaki Campbell duck: Breed info, pictures, traits & care guide. Pet Keen. https://petkeen.com/khaki-campbell-duck/

Hess, T., & Griffler, M. (2018, April 3). Potential duck health challenges. The Open Sanctuary Project; The Open Sanctuary Project, Inc. https://opensanctuary.org/common-duck-health-issues/

Hess, T., & Griffler, M. (2018, March 7). Welcome to waterfowl: The new duck arrival guide. The Open Sanctuary Project; The Open Sanctuary Project, Inc. https://opensanctuary.org/new-duck-arrival-guide/

Hess, T., & Griffler, M. (2023, May 26). How to conduct a duck health check. The Open Sanctuary Project; The Open Sanctuary Project, Inc. https://opensanctuary.org/how-to-conduct-a-duck-health-examination/

Holley, M. (2020, April 19). Raising ducks - pros and cons of backyard ducks. Outdoor Happens. https://www.outdoorhappens.com/raising-ducks-pros-and-cons-of-backyard-ducks/

How do ducks communicate? (2019, November 23). Sciencing; Leaf Group. https://sciencing.com/ducks-communicate-4574402.html

How to store duck eggs (step-by-step guide). (2022, October 2). Homestead Crowd | Homesteading, Gardening, Raising Animals Tips; Homestead Crowd. https://homesteadcrowd.com/how-to-store-duck-eggs/

Human-imprinting in birds and the importance of surrogacy. (n.d.). Wildlifecenter.org. https://www.wildlifecenter.org/human-imprinting-birds-and-importance-surrogacy

Indian Runner duck characteristics, uses & origin. (2021, May 31). ROYS FARM. https://www.roysfarm.com/indian-runner-duck/

Jagdish. (2022, August 10). How to start duck farming from scratch: A detailed guide for beginners. Agri Farming. https://www.agrifarming.in/how-to-start-duck-farming-from-scratch-a-detailed-guide-for-beginners

Khaki Campbell ducks: Characteristics, origin, uses. (2021, May 31). ROYS FARM. https://www.roysfarm.com/khaki-campbell-duck/

Kim, J. (2022a, August 26). Muscovy duck: Facts, uses, origins & characteristics (with pictures). Pet Keen. https://petkeen.com/muscovy-duck/

Kross, J. (2022). Waterfowl vocalizations. Ducks.org. https://www.ducks.org/conservation/waterfowl-research-science/waterfowl-vocalizations

Lazzari, Z. (2011, May 30). When & how to collect duck eggs. Pets on Mom.com; It Still Works. https://animals.mom.com/when-how-to-collect-duck-eggs-12546035.html

Lee, A. (2023, May 28). Decoding duck behavior: A guide for duck owners. Farmhouse Guide; April Lee. https://farmhouseguide.com/decoding-duck-behavior/

Lee. (2020, October 15). How to butcher a duck – a step-by-step picture tutorial. Lady Lee's Home; Lady Lees Home. https://ladyleeshome.com/how-to-butcher-a-duck/

Lesley, C. (n.d.). Hatching duck eggs: Complete 28-day incubation guide. Chickensandmore.com. https://www.chickensandmore.com/incubating-duck-eggs/

Lesley, C. (n.d.-a). Indian runner Ducks for beginners (the complete care sheet). Chickensandmore.com. https://www.chickensandmore.com/indian-runner-duck/

Lesley, C. (n.d.-b). Khaki Campbell duck: Care guide, size, eggs, and more.... Chickensandmore.com. https://www.chickensandmore.com/khaki-campbell-duck/

Lie-Nielsen, K. (2020, September 7). Ducks & geese are great permaculture livestock. Hobby Farms. https://www.hobbyfarms.com/ducks-and-geese-great-permaculture-livestock/

Liz. (2016, May 4). How to make a duck house. The Cape Coop. https://thecapecoop.com/make-duck-house/

Liz. (2016, September 28). Understanding backyard duck behavior. The Cape Coop. https://thecapecoop.com/understanding-backyard-duck-behavior/

Mallard duck nests. (n.d.). Wildlifecenter.org. https://www.wildlifecenter.org/mallard-duck-nests

Mallard life history. (n.d.). Allaboutbirds.org. https://www.allaboutbirds.org/guide/Mallard/lifehistory

Mccune, K. (2021, May 16). What is the best bedding to use for ducklings? Family Farm Livestock. https://familyfarmlivestock.com/what-is-the-best-bedding-to-use-for-ducklings/

Molly. (2022, July 19). Indian Runner ducks: Personality, appearance, and care tips. Know Your Chickens. https://www.knowyourchickens.com/indian-runner-ducks/

Muscovy duck: Characteristics, diet, uses, facts. (2021, May 31). ROYS FARM. https://www.roysfarm.com/muscovy-duck/

New Life on a Homestead. (2022, November 3). Top 10 duck keeping questions answered. Backyard Poultry. https://backyardpoultry.iamcountryside.com/poultry-101/top-10-duck-raising-questions-answered/

(n.d.). HGTV; Discovery UK. https://www.hgtv.com/outdoors/gardens/animals-and-wildlife/plants-toxic-to-backyard-ducks

Perez, S. (n.d.). Keeping Pet Ducks: Ducklings, Imprinting, and Ethical Treatment. Pethelpful.com. https://pethelpful.com/birds/Keeping-Pet-Ducks-and-Geese

Phillips, E. (2022, January 18). How to care for ducklings. Backyard Poultry. https://backyardpoultry.iamcountryside.com/poultry-101/how-to-care-for-ducklings/

Pierce, R. (2020, August 12). How to introduce new ducks to the flock. The Homesteading Hippy. https://thehomesteadinghippy.com/introducing-ducks-to-the-flock/

Pierce, R. (2022, September 17). Common duck diseases and how to prevent them. The Happy Chicken Coop. https://www.thehappychickencoop.com/duck-diseases/

Pierce, R. (2022, September 30). Free-range ducks: Pros and cons. The Happy Chicken Coop. https://www.thehappychickencoop.com/free-range-ducks-pros-and-cons/

Pierce, R. (2022a, August 10). Aylesbury ducks - the ultimate duck breed guide. The Happy Chicken Coop. https://www.thehappychickencoop.com/aylesbury-duck/

Poindexter, J. (2016, August 28). 10 important things to consider when building a duck coop. Morning Chores. https://morningchores.com/duck-coop-considerations/

Raising meat ducks in small and backyard flocks. (n.d.). Extension.org. https://poultry.extension.org/articles/poultry-management/raising-meat-ducks-in-small-and-backyard-flocks/

Reddy. (2023, March 10). Frequently Asked Questions About Duck Farming. AgriculturalMagazine. https://agriculturalmagazine.com/frequently-asked-questions-about-duck-farming/

Rice and duck farming as a means for contributing to climate change adaptation and mitigation. (n.d.). Fao.org. https://www.fao.org/family-farming/detail/en/c/1618289/

Sachdev, P. (n.d.). Are there health benefits of duck? WebMD. https://www.webmd.com/diet/health-benefits-duck

Sam, & February 1. (2020, February 1). Duck egg carbonara. Our Modern Kitchen. https://www.ourmodernkitchen.com/duck-egg-carbonara/

Sargent, A. (2020, November 28). Everything you ever wanted to know about duck eggs. Crooked Chimney Farm, LLC. https://crookedchimneyfarm.com/blogs/chickens-ducks/everything-you-ever-wanted-to-know-about-duck-eggs

Shaw, H. (2020, November 2). Duck fried rice. Hunter Angler Gardener Cook. https://honest-food.net/duck-fried-rice-recipe/

Shelton, L. (2023, March 13). Duck coops: 15 tips to design the perfect coop for your ducks. AgronoMag. https://agronomag.com/duck-coops/

Signs of malnutrition in birds. (2022, October 8). Petindiaonline.com. https://www.petindiaonline.com/story-details.php?ref=160503223

Steele, L. (2022, December 19). Types of ducks for eggs, meat, and pest control. Backyard Poultry. https://backyardpoultry.iamcountryside.com/poultry-101/types-of-ducks-for-eggs-meat-and-pest-control/

Stockman, F. (2019, June 18). People are taking emotional support animals everywhere. States are cracking down. The New York Times. https://www.nytimes.com/2019/06/18/us/emotional-support-animal.html

Stone, K. (2019, November 18). Commercial vs. Home mixed feed: Helpful answers for you. Stone Family Farmstead; Kristi Stone. https://www.stonefamilyfarmstead.com/commercial-vs-home-mixed-feed/

The DOs and DON'ts of feeding ducks. (n.d.). Friscolibrary.com. https://friscolibrary.com/blogs/post/the-dos-and-donts-of-feeding-ducks/

The Happy Chicken Coop. (2022, September 26). Muscovy duck: Eggs, facts, care guide, and more. The Happy Chicken Coop. https://www.thehappychickencoop.com/muscovy-duck/

The hidden lives of ducks and geese. (2010, June 22). PETA. https://www.peta.org/issues/animals-used-for-food/factory-farming/ducks-geese/hidden-lives-ducks-geese/

Thrifty Homesteader. (2016, June 23). Want eggs? Get ducks! The Thrifty Homesteader. https://thriftyhomesteader.com/want-eggs-get-ducks/

von Frank, A. (2022, August 30). 11 things you should know before raising ducks. Tyrant Farms. https://www.tyrantfarms.com/10-things-you-should-know-before-you-get-ducks/

von Frank, A. (2022, November 1). Duck eggs vs. chicken eggs: how do they compare? Tyrant Farms. https://www.tyrantfarms.com/5-things-you-didnt-know-about-duck-eggs/

von Frank, A. (2023, February 2). Are ducks dirty? Top tips for keeping your duck areas clean. Tyrant Farms. https://www.tyrantfarms.com/are-ducks-dirty-top-tips-for-keeping-duck-areas-clean/

What do ducks eat? Tips and best practices. (n.d.). Purinamills.com. https://www.purinamills.com/chicken-feed/education/detail/what-do-ducks-eat-tips-and-best-practices-for-feeding-backyard-ducks

What ducks and geese are good for foraging? (n.d.). Metzerfarms.com. https://www.metzerfarms.com/blog/what-ducks-and-geese-are-good-for-foraging.html

What should I feed my ducks? (2018, November 9). Org.au. https://kb.rspca.org.au/knowledge-base/what-should-i-feed-my-ducks/

When do you need a vet? (2016, July 7). Raising-ducks.com. https://www.raising-ducks.com/when-do-you-need-a-vet/